Biblical Prophecy

HOLY SPIRIT
ESSENTIALS

Biblical Prophecy

LEARN TO DISCERN AND APPLY DIVINE PROPHECY

JACK DEERE

Chosen
a division of Baker Publishing Group
Minneapolis, Minnesota

© 2025 by Jack Deere

Originally published by Servant Publications in 2001. Revised by Regal in 2008.

Published by Chosen Books
Minneapolis, Minnesota
ChosenBooks.com

Chosen Books is a division of
Baker Publishing Group, Grand Rapids, Michigan

Printed in the United States of America

Library of Congress Cataloging-in-Publication Data
Names: Deere, Jack author
Title: Biblical prophecy : learn to discern and apply divine prophecy / Jack Deere.
Other titles: Beginner's guide to the gift of prophecy
Description: Minneapolis, Minnesota : Chosen, a division of Baker Publishing Group, [2025] | Series: Holy Spirit essentials | Previously published under title: The beginner's guide to the gift of prophecy.
Identifiers: LCCN 2025016492 | ISBN 9780800778385 paperback | ISBN 9780800778392 casebound | ISBN 9781493452330 ebook
Subjects: LCSH: Prophecy—Christianity
Classification: LCC BR115.P8 D44 2025 | DDC 234/.13—dc23/eng/20250708
LC record available at https://lccn.loc.gov/2025016492

Cover design by Christopher Gilbert, Studio Gearbox

Baker Publishing Group publications use paper produced from sustainable forestry practices and postconsumer waste whenever possible.

25 26 27 28 29 30 31   7 6 5 4 3 2 1

CONTENTS

PREFACE

This book is a practical, simplified guide to contemporary prophetic ministry. Much of it is a telling of my own prophetic experience and my own encounters with the prophets. No contemporary prophetic ministry is perfect; no one ever acquired prophetic skill without blunders along the way. Only one Person ever had a perfect ministry, and even He learned obedience through suffering.

I offer clear scriptural references to support what I present in these pages. In the few places where I could not find unambiguous biblical support for something common in contemporary prophetic ministry, I have tried to indicate that.

I hope no one will be offended by my use of the word "prophet" throughout, rather than the more cumbersome "prophet and prophetess." Women are prophets, too, and I hold prophetic women in high esteem.

Finally, this book tells only the personal part of prophetic ministry, the basics to help you get started.

ACKNOWLEDGMENTS

Special thanks to Ken Gire, my friend and one of the most skillful writers I know, who read the entire manuscript and offered many valuable suggestions. I also have the proud father's pleasure of thanking my son, Stephen Craig Deere, an award-winning journalist, who also made significant improvements to this book with his own deft touch. And finally, thanks to the wonderful folks at Servant Publications, who originally published the book, especially Kathy Deering, my editor.

ONE

How It All Began

I wondered, *Did God bring me here, or did the devil bring me?* How did this man I had never met know my painful secrets? What good could come from revealing pain that I had hidden? Yet I had given the prophet permission to begin. Now I could not stop him!

Until that day, I had never met a prophet outside the pages of the Bible. I did not believe prophets *existed* outside its pages. To me, the prophets were just a temporary substitute until the Bible came along.

But then, a friend told me that there were *real* prophets in Kansas City. He was going to meet them, and he asked if I wanted to join him. I called my spiritual mentor to tell him I was going to meet these prophets. I knew no one more experienced in the supernatural ministry of the Holy Spirit than my mentor. I knew no one with a kinder spirit. And he said, "Jack, don't let them deceive you. God gave you a mind. Use it."

His warning put up my shield of determination not to be deceived. But my shield would not protect me—I was doomed. Not because I was about to face controversy. I was doomed because I would never again be happy in ministry unless it was infused with prophecy. The mind God had given me was no match for the prophetic heart He revealed to me!

So, one sunny September afternoon, with guarded heart and skeptical mind, I first met the pastor of these modern prophets. He radiated joy! Before I knew it, I wanted this man's joy and passion for God.

But I remembered that I had come to meet prophets, and I put on a superior attitude, determined not to be deceived. I was ready to meet these so-called prophets. My wife, Leesa, and I were led into a dingy little room with green carpet and orange plastic chairs arranged in a circle. My friends who had come with us wanted to encounter God. But I wanted to evaluate men.

I was met at the door by a tall man, dressed like an Eddie Bauer model. With graying hair, a salt-and-pepper beard, and deep-set eyes, he looked otherworldly.

Then he spoke: "Oh, I didn't expect to see you here."

Pretty cocky, I thought. Already I did not like him. "What do you mean? I don't even know you," I said.

"Well, I know you! Eight nights ago, I had a dream that woke me at three in the morning. I thought it was important, so I wrote it down. You were in the dream. Would you like me to tell you what the Lord showed me about you?"

"Yes," I said. I thought, *Take your best shot. I'm not going to be deceived. I have been warned about you prophets!* I was then in a completely different tradition of Christianity, and he really did not know me.

I knew about "cold reading." By careful observation, skilled people can "read" you, noticing behaviors. Gamblers call these signs "tells" because they tell something about you. Cold readers also get you to tell details in a way that makes it look as if those details have been supernaturally revealed. I knew that no matter how skilled this guy might be, I would give him no signs to read, no tells to help him win this game. I hardened my face like stone.

We stared straight into each other's eyes. My eyes revealed nothing. Then he spoke, and revealed everything.

"You have a prayer," he said in a soft Southern accent. "It's one of the major dreams of your heart." Then he told me the prayer I had prayed that very morning. I prayed it almost every morning. And he was right. It was the dream of my heart. "God said to tell you this dream is from Him and that you will get what you're asking for."

At the time, it was the biggest thing I could think to ask for. And this prophet was telling me my dream and that it would come true! But my granite face did not crack. He was getting no clues from me. Yet inside, my heart was exploding with joy. It took a superhuman effort not to cry. *How could I be so special to God that He would put such a dream in my heart and then tell me He would make it happen?*

Next subject.

"You had a father who dropped the ball on you," the prophet went on.

No! Not my father! How could he know about my father? How could he talk so calmly about the defining pain of my life? If I admitted what I was feeling now, I might destroy the "self" I had worked so long and hard to build. My fears kept me staring blankly at the prophet.

My father *had* dropped the ball on me, on all of us. Once a normal middle-class family of six, I went along with my two little brothers and sister to play at our grandmother's house one morning. Mom went to work at her insurance office. My father stayed at home. Sometime that afternoon, in the living room of our little three-bedroom house, my father put a gun to his head and ended the war raging within him. That night, my mother went to bed a 34-year-old widow with an eleventh-grade education and four small children to raise.

I was the oldest. I had just turned twelve. Beyond some friends who brought meals, no one helped us understand or heal. My father had been my hero. He was strong and he was smart. Life without him was unimaginable. That's probably why I never really grieved. To grieve, you must face the reality of your loss, and that was too scary.

No one was there to tell me that you couldn't heal unless you grieved. God was there, but it never occurred to me to pray to Him. He wouldn't give me my father back, so what was the use of asking? Pain and confusion puddled in my heart. I vowed to be strong, never to need anyone again. That reservoir of pain, hidden from me by my vow, did what all unhealed pain eventually does: It turned into bitterness. Long after I had ceased to feel the pain, the bitterness that I could not feel fueled all kinds of wild behavior.

But when I was 17, the Lord reined me in before I killed myself trying to gain the admiration of my friends. Overnight, I became a follower of Jesus. Overnight, I lost my wildness. But I did not lose the bitterness. I did not even know to talk about it to Jesus.

Nobody ever told me about bitterness. Nobody ever told me that even after you become a Christian, bitterness does not go away automatically. Nobody ever told me that bitterness can make you skeptical of goodness in others, even skeptical of God's goodness. Nobody ever told me that bitterness can make you afraid to love, for fear you will be cheated again. Nobody ever told me that the bitterness of your youth can hound you all the way to the grave. Nobody ever told me that if you don't remove the bitterness, it will integrate itself into your personality: You won't even know it is there—and you will deal with the anger and harshness, but never with the root.

So now, when I was the age of 38, Jesus decided that it was time He told me. He started by talking to me about the death of my father, when the spiritual acid first began to pool in my 12-year-old heart. He sent this preppy prophet to begin the conversation. I had no idea what the Lord was doing. I wasn't even sure it was the Lord. All I knew was that the prophet was bringing up something wrong that could never be made right. I wanted the conversation to end.

But his soft Southern voice continued: "The Lord is going to make up the loss of your father to you. He will send you new fathers. You won't learn from just one man. You will have the father you need for each new stage in your life."

His bringing up my father's death pained me, but the promise of new fathers bewildered me. How could God make up for the loss of my dad? I didn't need new fathers. I was totally happy with my spiritual mentor. But I sat with an unflinching stare.

Next subject.

"When you were young, the Lord gave you athletic ability, but He allowed you to be frustrated in the use of it. This was so you would put all your effort into cultivating the intellect. You've done that, but it hasn't brought you what you expected, and you're heartsick."

He could not have been more accurate! I was born with athletic ability. In Little League, I could play every position. I batted in the top four. I played tackle football with no pads. But at the start of seventh grade, I lost my father. Everything changed.

There was no one to take me to practices. My mother worked late into the evenings, selling insurance to keep her four kids fed and clothed. Sports were not necessities. Instead, I learned how to make the evening meals, and I missed out on the next three years of sports.

Sports were the most important thing in life. In those days, it was the way you proved that you were *somebody*. If you were a good athlete, you didn't have to be funny, smart, or wild. You had it made.

When I started high school, I could play sports again. I made the football and baseball teams my sophomore year. Then an ankle injury put me on the sideline. I gave up on athletics.

I gave in to a lifestyle of drunken recklessness. That's when the Lord saved me—literally—in the fall of my junior year. After that, I started reading—the Bible, C. S. Lewis, everything. And I never stopped. I found out that I could make straight A's when I wanted to. I also found out that there was an advantage to being perceived as smart. And the older you got, the greater the advantage became.

By the time I entered seminary, I had discovered that Greek, Hebrew, and other languages were easy for me to learn. In seminary, no cared who had played sports. But everyone knew the A-students.

Throughout my academic training, I was treated differently from those whose grades were lower. Doors opened for me. After the first year of my doctoral program, I "made the team." Two Old Testament professors took leaves of absence. I was picked to fill in.

"Professor Deere."

That was better than batting cleanup.

I was a professor. And not just any professor; I was a professor of theology, and of Old Testament exegesis and Semitic languages. As a result, people treated me with a new level of respect. Nobody ever told me it was dangerous to be a young professor. And no one ever told me that if you tried to find your identity in being theologically smart, you would wind up heartsick. No one, that is, until now.

The prophet was right. I *was* heartsick. But I hid it—from everyone. I continued to stare nonchalantly at him.

The Southern accent, now almost soothing, started again on the same theme: "All of that frustration was necessary to prepare you to fulfill the call that God has on your life."

A purpose behind the heartsickness! The mercy of God was inviting me to travel a new road. He had a call on my life, and everything so far was just preparation. Just as God would not let me succeed on an athletic field, neither would He let me die drunk in a car wreck. He let me succeed in academics, but He would not let me remain intoxicated by that success. He sent heartsickness to warn me of building my identity on academics.

I suddenly felt relief over my athletic failure. It would never haunt me again. I was never *supposed to* excel in sports! God had something more excellent for me. Faith and hope danced together joyfully in my heart. But I sat stoic, still staring.

Next subject.

"You're in a conflict right now, and you think there are only three people on your side. The Lord says to tell you that there are five more on your side."

I *was* in a conflict, and I *did* think only three people stood by me. Besides me, the only one who knew about this was Leesa! *How did he know this? How did he know any of these things?*

I was astounded. He was a real prophet. And God is a real God. And that day, I heard the voice of my Captain in those prophetic words. He was telling me that *He* would lead me through the minefields of this conflict.

By now, I should have dropped to my knees. But I continued to look unimpressed by the Lord's loving omniscience.

Next subject.

The future. The prophet told of my future. These predictions were meant for me to ponder, not publish. Because these words were about the future, they could not yet be verified. But because he had every single key fact about my past correct and had given each one a meaningful interpretation, I believed his predictions.

Now the prophet was finished with me. There was no longer a reason to maintain my façade. He had told me the secrets of my heart. With each secret came a promise that gave me freedom from the past and hope for the future. The prophet was real!

I wanted to shout for joy to the Lord, but I simply said, "Thanks."

"You're welcome," he replied.

Next, he began to speak to my wife. He was just as accurate with her. But Leesa put up no shield. Only a few sentences brought tears streaming down her face. His soft Southern voice continued calmly right through her tears, healing and promising.

As we left the room, the pastor asked, "Was any of that accurate or meaningful to you?"

"All of it was right on the money. Couldn't have been more correct," I said.

"You've got to be kidding. I was watching your face the whole time. I was sure you thought it was a bunch of bull!"

"I had been warned."

"Oh, *now* I understand."

I walked out of that room elated. Prophets were indeed alive and well. I was in love with prophetic ministry!

I also made a more profound discovery that morning. I had worked so hard to overcome the pain of my past, to become somebody special. Others thought I was special, but I felt sick at heart. Then, through the words of the prophet, God's healing love came to me, *reinterpreting* my past, present, and future. God told the prophet all about my pain because God wanted me to know that He had always been there. Always. Watching over the little boy robbed of his father, watching over the frustrated athlete, watching over the drunken rebel, watching over the heartsick scholar. Why? *Because I was special to Him.*

I had preached that truth many times to others, without feeling it myself. Now I felt that I had always been special to God, and feeling this made me love Him even more. Through the prophet, God removed my burden of trying to be special. He was telling me that I had never needed to look beyond His love to be special. Divine romance had just sneaked back into my life, and its calling card was the joy I felt, but could not explain. I did not know it then, but now I know that mystery, wonder, and awe had all blissfully returned to my life through that prophetic encounter. Adventure had finally returned!

TWO

Discovering Your Gift

My father told me that there was a God and that He was omnipotent, omnipresent, and omniscient. Good theology. My father told me that God created us because He was lonely. Bad theology. My father told me that I could go to heaven if my good deeds outnumbered my bad deeds at the end of my life. Hopeless theology. That was the sum total of my God knowledge for my first seventeen years: I'd been created by a lonely God whose power I could not match and whose standard I could not satisfy. So why try to be good?

But just a few weeks past my seventeenth birthday, my friend explained that Jesus Christ was God's Son and my Savior—my only Savior, the only way I could ever go to heaven. If I would trust Him to forgive me and give me a new life, Jesus would come into my life and never leave.

"What if I stumble?"

"You will, but He won't."

"What if I leave Him?"

"At times you will, but He won't."

"Really?"

"He'll pick you up and bring you back."

"Really?"

"He'll never leave you or forsake you. The Bible says so."

"Thanks."

"Good night."

For the first time ever, I had hope. I stumbled through a silent prayer. I don't remember the words, but that prayer was my surrender. It was my trust that Jesus would never leave me or forsake me, no matter what I did. I fell asleep believing that somehow, He would make the wrong in my life right.

How Gifts Are Given

That night, Jesus gave me the gift of eternal life. The Holy Spirit also gave me a gift that night, but He did not tell me what it was. I was using the gift before I even knew what it was, before I even knew the Holy Spirit gave gifts! It was the gift of teaching. Teaching was not the only gift the Spirit would give me, but it took me twenty years to discover His other gifts.

One joke on me was that I used my spiritual gift of teaching to tell the Church that these gifts weren't given anymore, even while these very gifts lay dormant within me!

Here's what I've discovered about how the Spirit gives gifts:

Sovereign Impartation

A lady told me her terrifying dream: She saw a huge pit filled with poisonous snakes, where babies were playing on top of the snakes. She heard a voice say, "Get the babies away from the brood of vipers!"

The lady wanted to know what the dream meant. She had never heard the phrase "brood of vipers." I explained that this was Jesus' description of the religious leaders opposing Him (see Matthew 12:34; 23:33). Those leaders' religious poison kept people from absorbing the life of God. The vipers represented religious leaders.

The babies were new converts or those coming to church for the first time. Instead of being nursed by the milk of God's Word, they were being poisoned by the leaders of the church.

This same lady told me she was regularly having vivid dreams; they had started recently and without warning. She had not been praying for dreams. Neither had she prayed for impressions about people, which she was now beginning to have. The impressions were not based on her knowledge of individuals; they seemed to come from nowhere. Sometimes they seemed more like an inner voice. She had not asked for this. In fact, she was part of a church that opposed the gifts of the Holy Spirit!

I had some good news and some bad news for this lady. The good news was that she was being called into prophetic ministry. The bad news was that she was being called into prophetic ministry. One day she would rejoice in revelation, and the next, both she and her friends would question her sanity. And on all days, the brood of vipers would have it in for her.

Sometimes prophetic gifts begin like this. The Lord just turns on the tap. He pours mystery and adventure back into our lives so that we may live in that realm where all things have become new (see 2 Corinthians 5:17).

The text that describes this sovereign impartation is 1 Corinthians 12:11: "All these [spiritual gifts] are the work of one and the same Spirit, and he distributes them to each one, just as he determines." The Holy Spirit has sovereignly given spiritual gifts to every believer in the Body of Christ so that we may better serve one another, and in so doing, bring glory to God (see 1 Peter 4:10–11).

Apostolic Impartation

The apostle Paul told Timothy "to fan into flame the gift of God, which is in you through the laying on of my hands" (2 Timothy 1:6). The word translated "gift" in this passage refers to spiritual gifts. Paul wrote to the Christians at Rome, "I long to see you so that I may impart to you some spiritual gift to make you strong" (Romans 1:11). Paul had authority to impart spiritual gifts not given at the time of someone's conversion.

Today, we have some leaders who carry more authority than others. They may have apostolic functions. When they are led by the Lord to lay hands on someone and pray for gifts, people can receive spiritual gifts, or their gifts can increase in strength.

John Wimber, who led the Vineyard movement, had authority to impart spiritual gifts. John laid his hands on me and prayed that healing and word of knowledge gifts in me would increase. The next day, I left on a ministry trip to another country. In one of the ministry trip meetings, I saw a man who appeared to be in his early sixties. I "knew" he feared getting Alzheimer's. I don't know how I knew his fear. I did not have a vision or hear an inner voice, but the second I noticed him, I knew the fear of Alzheimer's tormented him. This had never happened to me.

"Sir, do you have a fear of getting Alzheimer's?" I asked.

"Well, I suppose everyone has a fear of getting old," he replied.

"But do you think you are destined for Alzheimer's?"

"Yes. Yes, I do," he finally admitted. He had not told anyone about his secret torment. But God knew, and He stopped the torment through a prophetic word and prayer.

This happened to me often on that trip. The impartation I received from God's Spirit through the laying on of hands gave me a new level of revelatory and healing gifts.

Prophetic Impartation

Timothy must have received another spiritual gift sometime after his conversion, because Paul told him, "Do not neglect your gift, which was given you through prophecy message when the body of elders laid their hands on you" (1 Timothy 4:14).

I have seen prophetic gifts given or activated in this way many times—with the laying on of hands, and sometimes just through a simple word from a prophet.

22

Personal Prayer for Gifts

Some feel that because the Holy Spirit gives gifts "just as He wills," it is useless to pray for gifts. God does *everything* just as He wills (see Ephesians 1:11). But this does not mean that our actions have no effect on God. We can grieve God, and we can delight God (see Ephesians 4:30; Psalm 147:11). Jesus said, "If you believe, you will receive whatever you ask for in prayer" (Matthew 21:22). James said, "You do not have because you do not ask God" (James 4:2). Ultimately, the reconciliation of divine sovereignty and effective human prayers is a mystery. So pray for the gifts you want! You don't know how your prayers will affect the Holy Spirit's desire to give you gifts.

The same apostle who wrote that the Holy Spirit gives gifts "just as he determines" also encouraged his readers to pray for an interpretation if someone speaks in tongues (see 1 Corinthians 14:13), both tongues and interpretation also being spiritual gifts (see 1 Corinthians 12:10). God answers prayers today for spiritual gifts. If you want the gift of prophecy, pray for it. The following section will help you know if you have received a prophetic gift.

Recognizing Prophets

Three revelatory abilities mark the ministry of prophets:

1. They can accurately predict the future. Both Joseph and Agabus knew that worldwide famines were coming (see Genesis 41:25–32; Acts 11:27–28).
2. They can reveal to us the Lord's present priorities for our lives. For example, they may know when we should or should not fast (see Joel 1:14; 2:12, 15; Mark 2:18–20). They help us to discover the ways in which we may please the Lord in the present moment (see Ephesians 5:10).
3. They can shed light on the mysteries of our lives or make sense of our pain. For instance, Isaiah knew why some righteous

people die before their time (see Isaiah 57:1). Sometimes prophets can tell us why our religious practices are ineffective (see Isaiah 58:3–6; Jeremiah 14:12; Zechariah 7:4–7).

In short, prophets tell us the things we cannot know except by revelation from God. The goal is to encourage, comfort, and strengthen us so that we can marvel at the splendor, power, goodness, and wisdom of Jesus. It all goes back to Him!

Recognizing Your Gift

Some of us need to learn how we are *not* gifted before we can discover how we *are*. God can use the frustration of failure to purify our motives for ministry. Any Christian can prophesy without being a prophet, just as one can lead someone to Christ without being an evangelist. A prophet is someone who prophesies consistently and accurately. The occasional use of a gift may lead us to falsely conclude that it is our main gift, but if we habitually try to minister from the wrong gifting, frustration and failure are inevitable.

One way to recognize a gift is that we don't have to work hard to make it happen. Prophets don't have to strive for revelation; it simply *comes to them*. If they wait on the Lord, it increases. The same is true for evangelists, teachers, administrators, and healers. Gifts, by definition, are *given*, not worked up!

There are other clues to discovering our gifts. But first, let's look at a common mistake people make when they try to discover prophetic gifts.

A False Clue

"I'm called as a prophet," the young man said.

"How do you know?" I asked.

"Because I see what is wrong with people and ministries."

"I'll bet your gifting has brought you a lot of joy."

"No. The people I've ministered to don't understand. They get offended at the word of the Lord. What do you think is wrong?"

The young man may have had a prophetic calling, but he had missed the point of prophetic ministry. His misunderstanding led to a joyless, strife-filled life. Seeing what is wrong with people is not a gift. He had modeled his prophetic ministry after Old Testament prophets who expressed God's holy anger toward corrupt leaders and a rebellious people.

God is still angry with rebellious leaders (just read Matthew 23), but faultfinding and anger are not the signs of a prophetic calling. Rather, they show a wounded heart possibly full of bitterness. A New Testament prophet is called primarily to *build up*, not to tear down. A true prophetic gift is not simply being able to see what is wrong with people; it is seeing how to build them up. Anyone can make people feel guilty, but imparting grace and mercy requires a gift. The gift fills both the hearers and the prophet with divine joy and faith.

After my first encounter with a prophet, I walked out of the room dazzled by the omniscience, wisdom, mercy, goodness, and love of God. I was filled with joy. My faith went off the charts. My passion for the Lord increased. An angry person could not have led me to repentance. Instead, God fascinated me with His wisdom and dazzled me with His love. That revelatory encounter made sin so much less interesting!

Are You Called?

Here are some ways to find out if God is calling you to that kind of ministry:

The desires of our heart

One of the most common ways that God leads us is through our desires. But some Christians believe that God's will involves only going where you do not want to go, doing what you do not want to do, and being what you do not want to be. This is a lie of the enemy!

The Bible promises, "Take delight in the LORD, and he will give you the desires of your heart" (Psalm 37:4). If the Lord is the center of our joy, then we can trust our hearts' desires to lead us. Do you desire a prophetic gifting? Are you delighting in the Lord? If so, your desire is a sign that He is leading you into a prophetic ministry. Do not be afraid to follow that desire. If His yoke really is easy and His burden really is light, His gift may challenge you, but it will also speak to your deepest self.

The counsel of others

When God came to me through prophecy with His healing love, I wanted the gift of prophecy. But I lacked the confidence to pursue prophecy for my own ministry. The book of Proverbs affirms that God may use our friends to lead us: "Plans fail for lack of counsel, but with many advisers they succeed" (Proverbs 15:22). God also sent me many unsolicited and convincing prophetic words from people who did not know me, to encourage me to pursue both prophetic and healing ministries.

Ask those who really know you what they think about your gifting. And don't be afraid to ask prophetic people to pray for you.

Trying it out

If you regularly have prophetic experiences, this indicates a prophetic gifting. You may know things about others without being told. You may hear a voice, fall into a trance or, like Ezekiel, be transported to another place in a vision. These experiences may cause you to think you are going crazy. Of course, that's possible! But if the Lord is the center of your life, it is more likely that He's bringing you a prophetic gift.

Test the accuracy of your words. See whether they build others up when you attempt to minister prophetically. Most of all, try to listen to the Lord and obey Him by speaking His words. Explore your gifting with a few like-minded friends. Join a home group committed to training people in the gifts. A group with a godly leader submitted to the authority of the church's leaders is the perfect place to begin.

When I lead a home group like this, we spend fifteen or twenty minutes worshiping God. Then I usually teach for fifteen minutes on equipping for ministry. Next, we ask the Lord to guide us in ministering to one another. Someone might have a vision or an impression. A relevant Scripture might come to mind that leads us to pray for a specific person. Often, we are led to pray for healing, guidance, the release of gifts, or other practical things. We might have a time of sharing before we end the meeting by praying for the individuals singled out through the prophetic words. Some of the most exciting things happen after the meeting is over. (One thing I love about these meetings is that I never know what's going to happen. God's kindness and mercy continually surprise me!)

Because of God's kindness and mercy, we do not have to worry about discovering our gifts. The Giver has promised that those who seek will find. Our search is only a response to His longing for us. Whether we are eight years old or eighty, God wants to make prophets out of some of us, but He wants to make friends out of all of us—friends who are fascinated by the mystery and adventure of His holy love.

THREE

Learning How God Reveals

With a whispered secret, her healing began.

She was in her early twenties, with long blond hair and sad eyes. It was her first time at our church. Standing among those who had come forward for prayer, I prayed for God to heal her of a chronic physical ailment. Nothing happened. I prayed again. Still nothing. Then a young man named Carl whispered her secret to me.

Carl was a new Christian who was learning to pray for the sick. He whispered, "Ask her if she feels like God won't heal her because of the abortion she had when she was eighteen."

I thought, *No way I'm going to ask a total stranger such a personal and painful question!*

Then I thought about how Carl had demonstrated prophetic gifts. What did she have to lose if Carl were wrong? What did she have to gain if Carl was *right*? There was only one way to find out—obey!

"Forgive me if this is off-the-wall or too invasive," I said to the young woman, "but are you feeling like God won't heal you because of the abortion you had when you were eighteen?"

Her face told me the answer. She began to sob. Her unhealed pain came from something she thought could never be made right. She had kept her secret; it was always there inside her, spoiling every joy, whispering that she could never be forgiven, never be happy. Because she could not tell her secret, nobody ever told her that God longed to forgive her and set her free. Nobody ever told her that God thought about her every single day, longing to woo her with His love.

God had decided it was time to heal her heart, so He gave her secret to a very young prophet.

"How did you know? How did you know?" she sobbed.

"God told us."

She searched our faces, expecting to see condemnation. Instead, she saw faces enraptured with God's great love. Now it was her turn to be enraptured by that same love.

When she heard that God longed for her, that He was ready to forgive her right then, that He was ready to make her laugh again, and that Jesus had died for her to make all this possible, the condemnation was gone. She walked out of the church hopeful and happy, loved and forgiven. And it all happened through a revelation.

The Meaning of Revelation

Revelation is God making known to us what we did not know or could not have known through our natural senses.

Carl later told me that in his mind's eye, he saw a woman dressed in a long gown, standing on the young woman's shoulder and whispering in her ear that she could not be healed because of the abortion at age eighteen. Yes, I know that sounds weird. I don't have a biblical text for it.

I don't even have an interpretation of what Carl saw. God did not tell us more. And Carl did not add to it. Revelation is often like that. It answers a question you did not even know to ask—and raises new questions. All of us who want to follow God, especially prophets, should get used to walking in things not fully understood.

God may vary the clarity, intensity, or means of His revelation. When a Bible-times prophet said, "God spoke to me," he usually meant that the message from God was not mixed with the prophet's opinion or interpretation. He was speaking the words of God and nothing else. If the prophet said, "The hand of the Lord was upon me," he meant that the divine message was coming with greater power than usual (see Ezekiel 3:22). And if he said, "The Lord spoke to me with His strong hand upon me," he meant the message was impressed deep into his soul with compelling power (see Isaiah 8:11). But not all revelation comes with this force. Sometimes, the apostles said, "It seemed good to the Holy Spirit and to us . . ." (Acts 15:28).

It is always wise to be careful to indicate the level of certainty of a message. The Bible's authors did not always explain the words they used when they wrote about their prophetic experiences. Paul never defines the difference between a "word of knowledge," a "revelation," and a "prophecy." The good news is that we will learn more about revelation by looking at examples of how God spoke to the prophets than by trying to "define terms."

The Means of Revelation

How *did* God speak to the prophets? The primary way that God speaks to all believers is through the written Word of God, the Bible. The Bible has more authority than *any* present-day, personal revelation because its authority extends to all people everywhere, always. Prophets are obligated to study and meditate on the Scriptures just as much as teachers and other believers. But in addition to the Bible, prophets hear the voice of God through other means. Let's look at several of these now.

Appearances of the Lord

We read that no one can see God and live (see Exodus 33:20), yet He appeared to His friends and even to an occasional enemy (see Genesis 20:3). Sometimes, He appeared in a dream or a vision. Other times, He appeared in a physical form (see Genesis 18:1). Sometimes, He came as "the angel of the LORD" (Exodus 3:2). Other times, He came wrapped in His glory (see Exodus 16:10; 33:18–34:8). He appeared in moments of crisis, at turning points in history, to warn or to judge. Sometimes, He shared His plans or made a promise. If no one can see God, whom *were* these people seeing? It must have been the Son of God (see John 1:14–18).

One striking thing about these appearances is that they were not necessary. If God simply wanted to supply us with information, He could have sent angels. But God wanted to send His Son, His best.

It is like being in love: You long to be with the one you love. You want to do more than write letters—you want to go yourself, be close to that person. Behind these appearances to His people, we see God's heart burning with passion—His incomparable, radiant, holy love for us propels all forms of revelation! God loves us and wants to be with us. This is the greatest mystery I know. And the longer I ponder this mystery, the greater it grows.

One last point. If God appeared in His glory to grumbling, ungrateful Israelites (see Exodus 16:9–10), why wouldn't He appear today to people who are seeking Him with all their hearts?

Angels

Angels are "ministering spirits sent to serve those who will inherit salvation" (Hebrews 1:14). Angels protect us when we walk through fire, deliver us from the hand of the enemy, and bring messages to us from heaven. They escort us to heaven (see Luke 16:22). They may appear as guests in our home without ever revealing their real identity (see Hebrews 13:2). They may give no hint of their presence. Yet prophets often see angels when others cannot (see 2 Kings 6:15–17).

Recently, a godly prophetess whom I have known for years told me the following story. Lying sick on her bed in the afternoon, discouraged by what she saw as a lack of spiritual progress, this woman cried out to God to change her. Although her eyes were closed, she knew someone had entered the room, coming toward the bed. She was afraid to open her eyes. Then she felt the gentlest hands on her face, and one hand was laid across her forehead. She opened her eyes. Standing beside her bed was an elderly lady five feet tall, in a royal blue dress.

"Thank you," said the prophetess.

"If you are interested in changing, now is the time," said the lady, who then turned to look through the window. "I have to go now," she said, and floated through the ceiling.

This was a visitation, not a vision. The prophetess was wide awake during the whole experience, which lasted about a minute, and she felt immediate spiritual and physical effects after this encounter.

The next morning, the prophetess bounded out of bed at sunrise, filled with energy. The headache, sore throat, and tiredness that had harassed her for a week were gone. She was happy. She felt so special to God. He had sent an angel to touch her! Now she was confident that she could change and would change.

I believe the angel's message was not just for that prophetess, but also for all of us who want to change. *Now* is the time to change, to prepare for an outpouring of the Holy Spirit. In the Bible, encounters with angels increased just before turning points in the history of God's people. And maybe a turning point in *your* history lies just around the corner, through a touch by an angel or hearing the audible voice of God.

Audible voice

God spoke in an audible voice to individuals, to crowds, and even to a whole nation. Moses regularly heard the audible voice of the Lord (see Numbers 12:6–8). In Scripture, the audible voice of God comes in moments of crisis (see Genesis 22:11–12) or at great turning points, such as the giving of the Law at Sinai, the baptism and transfiguration of Jesus, the week before His cross, and the conversion of the apostle Paul.

All of us would like to have the clarity of an audible voice from God to guide us. But there is a price for that clarity. The original clarity and power of a revelation are meant to keep us from giving in to doubt during the trial that usually follows that revelation.

God still speaks in an audible voice. Nothing in Scripture teaches that God would stop speaking audibly once the Bible was completed. National church leaders from our own times report having heard the audible voice of the Lord. Although you might think God only speaks audibly to important church leaders, that is not the case.

Audible only to your ears

You may hear the voice of God with your ears when no one else does, even though someone might be standing beside you when His voice speaks. Samuel heard his name so loudly that he thought it must be Eli in the next room. He went to Eli, but Eli denied calling him. Finally, Eli realized that the Lord was speaking audibly to little Samuel but not to him (see 1 Samuel 3:1–14). Eli told Samuel what to say the next time the voice called him: "Speak, Lord, for your servant is listening" (verse 9). Samuel did this, and the Lord gave him his first prophecy.

The internal, audible voice

This internal voice of God is just as clear as the audible voice, only you do not hear it with your ears, but in your mind. In

Scripture, the phrase "the word of the Lord came to me saying" probably refers to His internal, audible voice. When some elders sat down before Ezekiel, "the word of the LORD came" to the prophet, giving him a message for them (Ezekiel 14:2). It does not appear that Ezekiel heard an audible voice. I have experienced this form of the voice many times, but it is the least common way that God speaks to me.

Sentence fragments

Maher-Shalal-Hash-Baz. What in the world does *that* mean? Isaiah didn't know either! But he was told to write it down (see Isaiah 8:1). These are four Hebrew words strung together in an ungrammatical sentence fragment. The words were just as clear as an audible voice, but their meaning was not. They contained a mystery.

Sometimes, God may speak only a single word. And while the word may be clear, its interpretation may not be. Why would God grant a clear revelation and then hide the interpretation? He does so for His own glory; our glory is to search out the meaning (see Proverbs 25:2).

The most profound truths are simple on the surface. Sadly, most of us stay on the surface. But when we leave superficial acceptance to surrender our heart to the contemplation of a truth, we journey into endless realms of mystery. Consider even the truth that God loves us. We all believe it, but what would happen to us if we plunged beneath the surface of this fundamental truth? What if we simply asked, *Why would God love me?*—and kept up the search until we got the answer?

To answer that question, we would have to think about God. To think accurately about Him, we would have to come into His presence. There, we would see His beauty, His splendor, and His holiness. The mystery of His love would only increase with each new revelation of Himself. As the mystery increases, so would our fascination. The more we love God for His own sake, the greater the glory we give Him. And the greater *our* glory—for in loving Him, we come to resemble Him more closely and to reflect more of His glory!

Every revelation to us from an infinite Person can never be more than a partial unveiling of the One who is drawing us after Him into eternal realms of mysterious beauty. That single word or sentence fragment from God that defies immediate understanding may have been sent to bring romance, mystery, and glory back into our relationship with Him.

A knowing

There are times when a divine revelation does not come as a voice or a spoken message. It may be something you simply *know*. And there may be no rational reason for how you know. When Jesus talked to the woman at the well, He knew she had had five husbands and was not married to the man with whom she was living (see John 4:18). On other occasions, the Bible simply says that Jesus knew someone's thoughts or plans (see Matthew 22:18; Mark 2:8; John 6:15).

After a church service, I frequently wait at the front of the auditorium with a ministry team to pray for people. I often know secrets about those coming for prayer. For example, a lady whom I had never met walked toward me. I knew she did not drink. I also knew she was certain she would end up an alcoholic. She had come to the front to get relief from chronic pain, not chronic fears, but her fear was on God's agenda for that day. When I asked her, she admitted that although she did not drink, she was certain she was destined for alcoholism.

Satan often torments people with these kinds of fears. That day, the prison of this lady's fears was opened, and she was set free. Jesus is the Knower of hearts, who reveals the secrets of our hearts to set us free from deception.

Impressions

An impression is a feeling that we ought to do something or that something is true. God uses impressions or feelings to guide us. Nehemiah said, "So my God put it into my heart to assemble the nobles . . ." (Nehemiah 7:5). From a biblical perspective, the heart is the center of the emotions and affections. Nehemiah followed a feeling in his heart, not an audible voice or a prophetic word. He assumed that this feeling came from God.

When Paul preached at Lystra, he "saw" that a lame man had the faith to be healed (Acts 14:9). You cannot physically *see* faith in someone; Paul had an impression. When Paul acted on it, the man was healed.

Dreams, visions, and trances

God uses dreams to speak to us in our sleep, when our defenses are down and we are more receptive. Visions are like dreams but normally occur while we are awake. Sometimes the Bible makes no distinction between dreams and visions; both terms describe the same experience (see Daniel 7:1–2). A trance is a vision in which we lose the use of our physical senses. Both Peter and Paul fell into trances (see Acts 10:10; 22:17). Although the Old Testament does not use the word *trance*, it appears that Balaam, Saul, and Daniel all experienced them (see Numbers 24:4; 1 Samuel 19:23–24; Daniel 10:9). Trances are not as common in the biblical record as dreams and visions are.

Job 33:14–18 tells us,

> For God does speak—now one way, now another—though no one perceives it. In a dream, in a vision of the night, when deep sleep falls on people as they slumber in their beds, he may speak in their ears and terrify them with warnings, to turn them from wrongdoing and keep them from pride, to preserve them from the pit, their lives from perishing by the sword.

This applies to the New Testament also, where dreams and visions occur throughout. The book of Revelation, for example, is an extended prophetic vision.

According to the Bible, dreams and visions are supposed to be a normal part of Church life. God speaks to many people in dreams and visions, and even more so to His prophets (see Numbers 12:6). We expect a sharp increase in God's use of these visionary experiences because, as Acts 2:17–18 relates,

> In the last days, God says, I will pour out my Spirit on all people. Your sons and daughters will prophesy, your young men will see visions, your old men will dream dreams. Even on my servants, both men and women, I will pour out my Spirit in those days, and they will prophesy.

Some prophetic dreams and visions may be simple and easy to understand. Others are complex and filled with symbolism. God may use a vision to take a prophet somewhere, such as when Isaiah was taken up to heaven for his commissioning (see Isaiah 6:1). Likewise, throughout the book of Revelation, John was taken to heaven and shown the last days. These experiences are so real that the prophet may not know if he is in his body or in a vision. When Paul was caught up into the third heaven, he could not tell if his journey was physical or spiritual (see 2 Corinthians 12:3). Many prophets today have had similar experiences, and some have them regularly.

Why does God speak to His people like this? Because there is more to us than just a mind. We have emotions that powerfully affect our behavior. Sometimes a picture is worth a thousand words. A graphic dream can shake us out of a complacent state. A vision of future joy may cause us to endure a present hardship.

We also live in a world filled with mystery. And although we are created in God's image, He is far more different from us than like us (see Isaiah 55:8–9). There are realms of truth and experience that transcend our understanding. God's visitations and visions allow us to experience these realms.

The natural world

God speaks to us through His creation in at least three different ways:

- The design and beauty of creation reveals the existence of a Designer who is both beautiful and powerful (see Romans 1:19–20).
- The natural world bursts with analogies to spiritual principles. For example, a lazy person may learn a great deal from observing the ways of the lowly ant (see Proverbs 6:6–11).
- God may illumine natural events to communicate His plans or express His ways. The Lord used a locust invasion to give Joel a message for his nation (see Joel 2:25–27). He used fire, wind, and an earthquake to get His point across to Elijah (see 1 Kings 19:11–12). God speaks to us through nature if we train our eyes to see, our ears to hear, and our hearts to receive.

Fleeces

To confirm God's will, Gideon laid out his wool fleece on a threshing floor and asked God to make it first wet and then dry (see Judges 6:36–40). It may be appropriate to lay out a metaphorical "fleece" when we must make a decision, especially when we have prayed and waited, but are still uncertain. Asking God for a definite sign of His direction is wise.

Three cautions regarding this:

- Be sure the "fleece" is supernatural and cannot be manipulated by anyone concerned.
- Use the fleece method sparingly. Don't take the view that God is your personal genie. That view will lead to a loss of intimacy with Him.

- Remember, this is a less personal form of revelation. Using a fleece says that either God has not spoken to you, that you could not hear Him, or that you don't have the confidence to act upon what He has already said.

Physical manifestations in our bodies

A sick lady touched the hem of Jesus' robe. He stopped to find this lady because He wanted her to know that it was her faith in Him, not any "power in His robe," that saved her (see Luke 8:43–48).

Today, God often speaks to prophetic people through bodily signs. One prophet I know feels a physical chill on his body in the presence of an AIDS victim. Sometimes when I speak, I feel a pain that is not mine. This helps me identify people the Lord may want to heal. As soon as I ask people having that kind of pain to come for prayer, the pain I feel leaves.

Physical manifestations are subject to abuse and fabrication. People who have them may feel superior to others. But remember, any good thing may be abused or counterfeited. We are more than our minds. Our bodies constantly tell us when to rest, when to eat, when to see a doctor, etc. We regularly use our bodies rather than words to communicate love, dislike, apathy, and many other things. So why should we think it strange if God uses our bodies to communicate with us? If you get physical signs in your body, learn what they mean. Don't abuse them, and don't make a big deal out of them.

The five spiritual senses

Biblical prophets could see things with their spiritual eyes and hear things with their spiritual ears. Visions are not seen with our natural eyes, and God's internal audible voice is not heard with our natural ears. But what about taste, touch, and smell? God speaks through these senses as well. First, if He speaks by spiritual seeing and hearing, we may expect Him to speak by the other senses as well, unless there is a reason why He wouldn't.

Second, beginning prophets as well as mature prophets are getting messages today through the spiritual senses of taste, touch, and smell. One lady I know frequently "smells" incest victims. When a victim of abuse walks by her, she often smells it. She then prays for an appropriate time to minister to the wounded one.

Third, since the devil counterfeits God's methods, the fact that there's a counterfeit assumes the existence of the real. (I have also been in the presence of demonic touch, smell, and taste when we have been casting demons out of people.)

A Word of Caution

People who want a supernatural ministry make these two common mistakes:

1.) To think that if an angel could just visit us, or if we could just hear the audible voice of God, or if we could just be caught up into heaven, all our problems would be solved and we would always have the faith to obey God. But Israel watched God send plagues and part a sea, saw His fiery glory, and heard Him speak. Yet these same people worshiped a golden calf idol with a sexual orgy when Moses was gone too long!

Moses himself, a great prophet, talked with God face-to-face, yet he disobeyed God and died outside the Promised Land. Elijah called fire down from heaven, but the next minute he was running for his life from Jezebel. Our humanness doesn't stop when we receive a gift. No spiritual experience eliminates our need to keep in step with the Holy Spirit and walk by faith.

2.) To become more enamored with supernatural experience than with the Lord Himself. This is especially common when we first begin prophetic ministry. If revelation and power don't lead us into deeper friendship with Jesus, we are focusing on the gift instead of on the Giver of the gift. Eventually, we will deceive ourselves and those who follow us.

Because the Father's holy love lies behind all revelation—sending it, protecting it, and interpreting it—we *must* become immersed in that love. For God will trust His secrets to those who love Him and love all that He has created.

FOUR

Discerning God's Voice

ou're going to die before your time." That's what the voice told her, over and over, for a long time. I also "heard" that voice as I looked at her section of the audience. But was it God trying to prepare her for an untimely death? Was it due to her mother's premature death? Or was it the voice of darkness itself: powerless to take life, but expert at defiling life?

The voice had power *because she believed* it was telling the truth. I believed the voice was lying. I pointed at her section and said, "Someone sitting here believes you are going to die before your time. But you're not. Would you please raise your hand? We want to pray for you."

As it turned out, she was not the only person who had been hearing this voice! I knew it was not God warning these people of an early death, and I knew that the power this voice had over them was supposed to end that night.

But how did I know? How do you know when God is speaking in your spirit?

Four Tests

God is not the only one who speaks to us. Our own thoughts and emotions speak to us. The pressure we feel from others speaks to us. The devil also speaks to us (see Revelation 12:10). All these voices! How can we discern whether it is God speaking?

Here are four tests to help you begin. But you will need to ask for discernment as well, another gift!

The Bible

The Bible is the first test through which everything must pass. If my impression contradicts the Bible, I discard it. Read the Bible. Know the Bible. Live the Bible. Don't speculate about things an omniscient God says you cannot know (see Matthew 24:36). Instead, pay close attention to what the Bible *does* say to attend to. Our first line of discernment is God's written Word.

When the apostle Paul came to Berea preaching Christ, for example, the Bereans "examined the Scriptures every day to see if what Paul said was true" (Acts 17:11). We are to follow the example of the noble Bereans.

You would think that Bible believers would never accept something as true if it contradicts the Bible, but they do it all the time. For example, young Christians marry unbelievers all the time, even though the Bible says not to do it (see 2 Corinthians 6:14). If we want something, we can decide we are an exception to the rule! Yet Jesus said, "The scripture cannot be broken" (John 10:35 KJV). Although God's voice may contradict my *interpretation* of Scripture, it will never contradict the Bible, no matter what my desire says.

The voice's character

Here is the rest of the story of the lady I told you about at the beginning of this chapter. For twelve years, she woke up every day thinking that she was supposed to die that day. It never occurred to her that the voice was the voice of the liar.

After I shared my impression, she came forward for prayer. "Do you think you are going to die prematurely?" I asked her.

"Yes. That's what I think God is telling me."

"Do you think your children are going to die young, too?"

"Yes," she said and burst into sobs.

"That's not God speaking to you," I told her.

"How do you know?"

"How does that voice make you feel?"

"Hopeless."

"That's why it can't be God. His words bring hope. How long has the voice been saying that you and your children are going to die soon?"

"Twelve years."

"That's *another* reason the voice is lying. Look how long you have lived already! Twelve years is not soon!"

I believe the lady was set free from the tormenting voice that night. The voice threatening a premature death is a common trap. Christians fall into this trap because we have not learned to recognize the character of our Lord's voice. It isn't as though He never tells people that they are close to death; He told the apostle Paul that the time for his departure had come (see 2 Timothy 4:6). But these words gave Paul joy and peace! God speaks encouraging words to His weak and immature children who may stumble, but stumble toward Him.

If we read the Bible with the illumination of the Holy Spirit, we will learn to recognize the character of the Lord's voice. When Jesus speaks to His followers, He does not condemn, nag, or whine. His voice is calm and authoritative. Even His rebukes bring hope.

If it is really the Lord speaking to us, it should bring peace if we truly listen (see James 3:17; Philippians 4:6–7; John 16:33). The voice of the devil accuses, confuses, and condemns, to steal our hope and faith (see again Revelation 12:10). Learn the character of each voice that speaks to you before you attribute it to God.

The voice's fruit

What kind of fruit does that inner voice produce when you follow it? Jesus said that we could tell the difference between false and true prophets by the fruit of their ministries (see Matthew 7:15–23). In the same way, if we are following the voice of the Lord, we will see the fruit of the Spirit in our lives.

Pay attention to the results of the different voices that you follow. Keep records. What happens when you follow the voice of anger? When you follow the voice of greed? When you follow the voice of fear? If we are following God's voice, submitted to Him and in step with His Spirit, we can expect good spiritual fruit, especially peace (see Philippians 4:9).

The voice's difference

There are two verses in the Bible that believers simply do not believe. I am referring to Isaiah 55:8–9: "'For my thoughts are not your thoughts, neither are your ways my ways,' declares the LORD. 'As the heavens are higher than the earth, so are my ways higher than your ways and my thoughts than your thoughts.'"

Most of us would say we agree with this passage, but we tend to agree with it by saying, "*They* don't think like *we* do, do they, Lord?" We tend to think it is the other people who don't understand God's ways.

Yet if God's thoughts and acts differ enormously from ours, these two realities then follow:

- The most important things in life *can be understood only by divine revelation*. Human intellect is not enough to understand God's ways.
- When God's revelation comes, it may seem wrong to us at first. When Jesus told the disciples that He would be crucified and raised three days later, Peter said, "Never, Lord!" It was not what Peter thought should happen. No matter

how many times Jesus told the disciples about the cross, they could not understand it. If His best friends did not understand His cross, what makes us think *we* can?

The cross of Jesus contradicted human wisdom and experience, and even the scholars' understanding of the Bible. After two thousand years, the cross is still a mystery that is only partially understood. As the mystery of the cross demonstrates, God comes to us in ways that are difficult to recognize and easy to reject. How could it be otherwise when our Creator is *infinitely superior* to us in every way?

Our inability to recognize God and His ways is one reason He sends us prophets. And if we want to *be* prophets, we must pay close attention to the thoughts that come to us out of nowhere with a message that contradicts our normal ways of thinking or acting.

These four tests—Scripture, and a voice's character, its fruit, and its difference or content—help us recognize God's voice. But nothing substitutes for experience. Through experience, we grow in our ability to hear God. "But solid food is for the mature, who by constant use have trained themselves to distinguish good from evil" (Hebrews 5:14).

Knowing *about* God's voice is not the same as knowing God's voice. How do you learn to know God's voice? Are you constantly talking to and listening to Him? It is through "constant use" that we grow in discernment and our ability to hear His voice. Talk to Him. Listen to Him. Often!

According to Jesus, all Christians can hear His voice (see John 10:27). But if you practice something, but neglect the foundational things, you can make wrong ideas permanent. So when it comes to hearing God's voice, the key lies not in the four tests, or even in good practice, but rather in our hearts! Neglecting our hearts is a sure way to being deceived. The key to hearing God lies not in our *intelligence*, but in our *humility*.

The Humble Heart

It is amazing that there are people whom God Himself esteems. But *who* He esteems is even *more* amazing. He esteems the humble. David says, "For the LORD is exalted, yet He looks after the lowly, but He knows the haughty from afar" (Psalm 138:6 NASB). God also declares, "These are the ones I look on with favor: those who are humble and contrite in spirit, and who tremble at my word" (Isaiah 66:2). Peter told us: "Clothe yourselves with humility toward one another, because, 'God opposes the proud but shows favor to the humble.' Humble yourselves, therefore, under God's mighty hand, that he may lift you up in due time" (1 Peter 5:5–6).

Scripture declares that humble people hear and understand the voice of God. Among all the Old Testament prophets, no one heard the voice of the Lord like Moses, for he was "more humble than anyone else on the face of the earth" (Numbers 12:3). Humility is a primary character quality of all great prophets—and the pathway to friendship with God. God deals with the proud at a distance, but with the humble it is up close and personal.

Jonathan Edwards said that the hardest sin to detect and the one that lies at the bedrock of most other sins is pride. If that's true, I wonder if humility is the most difficult virtue to acquire. Humility is the virtue to which our flesh is most opposed, since so many other virtues grow from it. Bottom line: Anyone famous for loving God will be exceptionally humble.

What Is Humility?

The dictionary tells us what humility is *not*: not proud, not arrogant, not haughty, not assertive, not pretentious. The Bible does not give a one simple definition of humility, but it gives numerous examples of humble people.

- Humble people are small in their own eyes. Consider John the Baptist. He knew he was special. His conception was announced by the angel Gabriel (see Luke 1:11–20). His birth was celebrated by powerful prophecy (see Luke 1:67–79). He knew that he was the "voice" talked of in Isaiah 40:3, the forerunner of the Messiah. John knew he was special, yet he was still humble. Compared to the Messiah, John said that he was not worthy even to take off the Messiah's shoes (see John 1:27). Jesus said that no one on earth was greater than John the Baptist (see Matthew 11:11). John embraced humility, even when it meant his ministry would diminish. He said of Jesus, "He must become greater; I must become less" (John 3:30). At the height of his popularity, John knew that Jesus' coming meant his ministry was ending. Humility is seeing ourselves *not in comparison with one another, but in the light of God's greatness.*

- Humble people put their confidence in the mercy of God rather than in their abilities or character (see Romans 9:15–16). Humility is knowing that our best qualities are not enough to deserve God's love. Jesus illustrated this in the story of the proud Pharisee boasting about his righteousness, contrasted with the sinner crying out for mercy (see Luke 18:9–14). It is all God's grace!

- Humble people are calm, because they know it is the Lord who determines the outcome (see Proverbs 21:31; 16:9, 23). When John the Baptist's disciples said that more people were going to Jesus than to him, the prophet replied, "A person can receive only what is given them from heaven" (John 3:27). Jesus reminded His disciples the night before His crucifixion, "Apart from me you can do nothing" (John 15:5).

- Humble people put their confidence in the Holy Spirit's ability to speak, not in their ability to hear. They put their confidence in Jesus' ability to lead, not in their ability to follow. At the end of his life, Paul said it like this: "The Lord will rescue me from every evil attack and will bring me safely to his heavenly kingdom" (2 Timothy 4:18).

- Humble people are willing to associate with and serve people of lower position (see Romans 12:10; Galatians 5:13; Philippians 2:3–4), just as Jesus and our Father do (see Philippians 2:5–11; Isaiah 57:15; 66:2).

- Humble people embrace their weaknesses. Paul tells us that the power of Christ rests on people who embrace their weaknesses (see 2 Corinthians 12:9–10). Weakness is our lack of ability to do something we consider necessary. The apostle Paul did not tell us what his weakness was, only that it tormented him (verse 7). Instead of being distressed by their weaknesses, humble people see that their weaknesses are opportunities for the power of Christ to rest on them.

Becoming Humble

If humility is so essential for hearing the voice of God, how do we get it? Not by reading about it! Here are some ways to become humble:

First, learn to rejoice in the pain.

"Son though he was, he learned obedience from what he suffered" (Hebrews 5:8). That is a very unexpected statement about Jesus! How did a perfect Person "learn" anything, especially obedience? Somehow pain was necessary, even for Jesus. If Jesus needed pain, how much more do we?

No one becomes humble without pain doing its work. Some preachers give us the idea that we suffer pain only because of our unbelief. Sometimes that's true. But it wasn't true of Job. It certainly wasn't true of Jesus! God could prevent *all* our pain if

He chose to, but instead He chooses to *use* our pain, giving us the opportunity to become humble—if we don't let the process produce bitterness.

Walk in the desert gladly.

Humility is almost always acquired in the hard times—the "desert experiences." Moses, David, John the Baptist, and Jesus all had them. Likewise, everyone greatly used by the Lord is led into the "desert" to get humility. The desert is necessary—because *no human being has the character to bear perpetual success*. Failure, pain, and dryness break the power of our pride. The desert is where we discover our absolute need of constantly walking close to Jesus in the Holy Spirit.

Prophetic ministry can be spectacular. Because of that, prophets easily become puffed up. The desert cures pride. The greater the gifting, the greater and more severe the time in the desert will be. Welcome the desert! It means the gift of humility is being imparted, and promotion or restoration is on the way.

The desert represents that time in our lives when we seem unproductive and God seems far away. And if that weren't enough, a major test is often thrown at us. It is where we learn that apart from Christ, we can do nothing.

Be with Jesus—and with others.

God made us to connect with Him and with others at the deepest level. Before Jesus called the apostles to build a ministry, He called them to be with Him (see Mark 3:13–15). Powerful ministries are built on a deep connection with God and with His people. Be glad to be with humble people. It is a law of human nature that we will become like our friends (see Proverbs 13:20).

All of us need several friends of the same gender who are so close that they know all our secrets. Why? Because if you can't talk about it, it owns you. When I share a dark secret with a close friend, half the power of it over me is broken. James said that if we want to be healed, it is necessary to confess our sins to one another (see James 5:16). You can only do this with people who would never use your secrets to betray you.

The best measurement of our love for God is our capacity to enjoy Him. The more we are "with" God, the more we enjoy Him. But it is so much easier to "do for" God than to "be with" God. We often crowd our lives with doing, so that that there is little left for being with God or with best friends. And yet these friendships give us real joy, allow us to feel significant, and transform us.

Humility is produced by pain, by being with Jesus, and by being with humble people. And we never "arrive." Becoming humble is a lifelong process (see Philippians 3:12–14).

FIVE

What Does God Mean?

*B*lood pressure.

From out of nowhere, those words entered my mind. I was looking at the crowd, praying for revelation. The woman at whom I was looking appeared perfectly healthy. Nothing suggested she had blood pressure problems. I had not been thinking about illnesses.

I often had experiences like this, what some call "words of knowledge." But the Lord was also going to give me a lesson about my heart and humility.

I was sure this was going to be impressive. From the stage, I asked the lady, "Do you have high blood pressure?"

"No," she replied.

What? I was sure the Lord had indicated her. Maybe it was someone in her family.

"Does anyone in your family have high blood pressure?"

"No."

Strike two. Maybe the revelation was for someone seated near her, and I just hadn't given the Lord time to indicate who it was.

"Does anyone seated around this lady have high blood pressure?" I asked that part of the audience.

Strike three. Embarrassed, I admitted my mistake and moved on.

After the meeting, the woman who did not have high blood pressure came up to me. She said, "You know, my husband has low blood pressure. It's so bad that sometimes he passes out. Do you think that might have been what you were seeing?"

Aha! I had made a beginner's error in prophetic ministry.

Revelation, Interpretation, and Application

The Lord's mercy is so great that nothing was lost that didn't need to be lost. I gained more by my mistake than I would have gained in success. You see, the Lord still allowed us to identify the problem so that we could pray for the lady's husband. His mercy redeems even our mistakes and makes us better.

And there was something I needed to *lose*. My first mistake took place in a hidden part of my heart. I had heard the words *blood pressure* in my mind. The revelation was true. But I *assumed* it meant high blood pressure—after all, high blood pressure is very common. The other assumption I made was that the revelation referred to the woman I was looking at when the word came into my mind.

Here is what I should have done: I should have asked the Lord what the word about *blood pressure* meant, and how it applied to this lady. If I had done that, but the Lord had not answered me, I could have asked her, "A moment ago, I was looking at you and the words *blood pressure* came to my mind. Do those words mean anything to you?"

Had I done this, she would have said, "They certainly do. My husband has low blood pressure. He even passes out from it!"

My mistake was this: I had failed to distinguish between revelation (what is said), interpretation (what it means), and application (what we do about it). These three factors matter every time God speaks to us.

The revelation—God's message—may come through the Bible, a dream, an impression, or in other ways. If the revelation is from God, then it must be true because God cannot lie (see Hebrews 6:18). However, we can have a true revelation and give it a *wrong interpretation*. Furthermore, we can have a true revelation, a correct interpretation, and a *wrong application*. If the message from the Lord is going to benefit someone, we need to be right at all three stages.

Even seasoned prophetic people can misapply a revelation. The prophet Agabus correctly heard the Holy Spirit say that when Paul went to Jerusalem, he would be imprisoned. But Paul's companions, including Luke and maybe even Agabus, urged him not to go. Paul went anyway (see Acts 21:10–14). The application for Paul was simply informational. He was not worried about imprisonment. He already knew he was supposed to go to Jerusalem, and this simply confirmed what would happen.

A helpful practice is to keep on distinguishing between the revelation, interpretation, and application. At every stage, keep asking God, *What do I need to know?*

Being Taught Humility

Can you see how important humility is in this process?

You may be wondering why God did not just say *low blood pressure* when He gave me that word. If He could suggest *blood pressure*, He could have added the word *low*. Even if I had not given the revelation a wrong interpretation, the question of why He didn't do that would still need an answer. And in that answer lies the key to interpreting *all* revelation.

I think God omitted the word *low* because He was teaching me humility. First, He was teaching me the habit of humble dependence on Him for everything. Second, He let me suffer a little healthy embarrassment.

You see, when the words *blood pressure* came to my mind, I experienced a surge of joy. I know part of that joy was the delight I always feel in the presence of expressions of God's omniscience—but *another* part of the joy came from anticipating how impressed the audience would be with my revelation!

"Knowledge puffs up" (1 Corinthians 8:1). No one is immune to the pride of knowledge. Knowledge in any form makes us impressed with ourselves. It is hard to let go of impressing others. But note this well: It does *not* impress the One who knows everything. He rather hopes that we use the knowledge He gives us to *impress people with His Son.*

My embarrassment gave me a gentle reminder not to be impressed with myself when the Holy Spirit shows me the secrets of His children. The embarrassment that the Lord engineered was a sign of His love and His commitment to instill humility in me.

Write It Down

Another helpful practice for understanding God's meaning in revelations is to follow Daniel's example. He wrote down his visions and dreams immediately after having them (see Daniel 7:1). We cannot interpret what we cannot remember. We can have the most vivid dream, but if we do not write it down within five or ten minutes after waking, most likely we will forget it quickly.

Visions and impressions can also be lost quickly, as well as insights gained from meditating on Scripture. I have developed the habit of writing down everything. This helps me accommodate the Lord's tendency to speak to me at unusual times—just to see if I want to hear Him!

For much of my Christian life, I expected God to speak to me only through the Bible, when I was studying it. I thought God would accommodate Himself to my schedule. It was not much like the way He spoke to people in the Bible, but it was convenient for *me.* I made notes during my Bible study, and God did speak to me. But I also missed a great deal because I restricted my listening to only one form of the Lord's communication, at one time of the day.

Although God was speaking to me at various times and in various ways, I ignored those ways because I thought they were unreliable. I thought they would distract me from the Bible. When I finally admitted that the way God spoke to people in the Bible was also the way He speaks to people today, I began to hear His voice more often. I now have a more intimate relationship with Him. Because of the intimacy in our relationship, I speak to Him often during the day, and He to me. He is not nearly so predictable as I imagined. And that discovery has made life with Him much more adventurous!

I keep paper, pen, and a recording device (nowadays, my phone) with me wherever I go and by my bed. If I wake up at 3:00 a.m. at the end of a vivid dream, I write it down. If an insight comes to me while I'm driving, I can record it. God often speaks to us during mundane chores. When He does that to you, stop and record it. This habit helps us meditate on what He says to us.

If we do not write down a revelation, we may lose the blessing that was meant for us and others. It may even cost us money, as it once did with me. During some mindless task, an impression came into my mind regarding a stock I owned. The impression was that the stock was going to triple in value, and when it did, I should sell it. I was sure this was from God. I did not write it down, but I did tell my wife. The stock tripled. I did not sell. I had forgotten! My wife reminded me of the impression after the stock price fell. She also reminded me to practice what I preach: Write it down!

The Role of the Heart

Writing down your revelations, as well as distinguishing between revelation, interpretation, and application, are helpful practices. Still, they don't get to the heart of interpretation.

According to the Bible, as far as human responsibility is concerned, the key to interpreting all forms of divine revelation is found in the heart, not in the mind. The religious leaders of Jesus' day studied what they had of the Bible more than anyone, but because of the condition of their *hearts*, they never heard God's voice (see John 5:37). Even when God spoke to Jesus in an audible voice, some people standing by Him heard only thunder, even though the voice had come for their benefit (see John 12:27–30). If our hearts are not right, we won't recognize God even when He speaks to us in an audible voice.

The Pharisees were arrogant. Their pride made it impossible for them to hear God's voice in *any* of the ways God was speaking at the time. On the other hand, Jesus was humble in heart (see Matthew 11:29) and never failed to hear God's voice. Humility, not intelligence, is the heart quality that moves God to speak and enables us to hear Him clearly. It is the humble, not the smart, whom God guides and teaches (see Psalm 25:9).

When it comes to understanding God's voice, three expressions of humility stand out. The humble want (1) to obey, (2) to be friends with God, and (3) to pray. Let's look at those three next.

Obedience

The religious leaders did not believe that Jesus was speaking God's words, so He gave them a way to discern the origin of His message. He said, "If anyone is willing to do His will, he will know about the teaching, whether it is of God, or I am speaking from Myself" (John 7:17 NASB).

Humble people want to obey God, even when obedience is painful. Our willingness to do whatever He tells us encourages Him to speak to us and enables us to recognize and understand His voice. One wise man said that we obey our way to understanding. Why should God speak to us if He knows we have no intention of obeying Him?

Friendship with God

Humble hearts want an intimate friendship with God. And they want that friendship more than they want a ministry. This is also what God longs for.

58

The Lord longs for friends with whom He can share His secrets. Abraham got so close to God that God did not want to do anything without revealing it to him first (see Genesis 18:17). *This closeness is the personal goal of prophetic ministry*, not the delivering of prophetic words. Powerful prophetic words are the *by-product* of being close friends with the most powerful Word of all.

Ministry can sidetrack. Someone has said that the greatest hindrance to *loving* God is *serving* God. I believe it! I ask myself often: *What is it I really want, a great following or a great friendship?* When I am really sidetracked, I forget to ask myself that question. But then God asks me. He seems determined to make a good friend out of me in spite of my being willing to settle for less. And I am sure He feels the same way about you.

Prayer

Humble people pray. Praying is one of the most practical things we can do, both to get revelation and to understand it. God told Jeremiah, "Call to me and I will answer you and tell you great and unsearchable things you do not know" (Jeremiah 33:3). How much revelation do we forfeit simply because we do not ask God to tell us "unsearchable things"? How much revelation do we fail to understand because we do not ask God to reveal its meaning?

When Daniel was meditating on Jeremiah's prophecy that Israel's captivity would last for seventy years, he prayed. An angel was sent to give Daniel "insight and understanding" (Daniel 9:22). Prayer allows us to search the depths of Scripture, as well as the meaning of visions and dreams.

Prophets have gifts to interpret revelation that occurs outside the Bible. Some of today's prophets have gifts like those of Joseph and Daniel, who interpreted not only their own dreams, but also the dreams of others. Some prophets are so gifted at interpretation that it seems effortless, but in the Bible, those who were skilled interpreters of revelation were people devoted to prayer.

In the third year of King Cyrus, Daniel had a vision so perplexing and horrifying that he mourned, fasted, and prayed over the vision for *three weeks*. At the end of the three weeks, an angel came to Daniel and said this:

> Do not be afraid, Daniel. Since the first day that you set your mind to gain understanding and to humble yourself before your God, your words were heard, and I have come in response to them. . . . Now I have come to explain to you what will happen to your people in the future.
>
> Daniel 10:12–14

This experience makes Daniel a model for all who want to understand the language of the Holy Spirit. The elements that unlock the meaning of revelation—humility, fasting, prayer, friendship with God, and willingness to obey God—are found in this chapter of Daniel.

The prophet was given a vision he could not understand. Instead of giving up, he "set [his] mind to gain understanding." He prayed and fasted until the interpretation came. When we pray and fast, we are confessing our weakness and expressing our dependence on God. Daniel had humbled himself before God. He had a friendship with God, for God "highly esteemed" him (Daniel 10:19). And Daniel was willing to do whatever was required to obey and to understand the vision.

Following Daniel's example is the best way I know to understand divine mysteries. But we know so little of God and His ways! Some things He will leave a mystery, regardless of our efforts to understand them. Don't be discouraged by this; a life without mystery is a dull life. And God promises to quell our anxieties with His peace (see Philippians 4:6–7)—when we will give them to Him. Remember this the next time the Lord speaks to you with a disturbing symbol.

The Purpose of Symbolic Language

"Unless you eat the flesh of the Son of Man and drink his blood, you have no life in you," said Jesus (John 6:53). Why would He use such outrageous symbolism? The crowd of disciples following Him did not appreciate it; they grumbled, "This is a hard teaching. Who can accept it?" (verse 60). And many of them deserted Him.

But why were they following Him in the first place? Jesus had said they were following Him for food (see John 6:26). That is the great temptation of religious people: to use God rather than love Him, following Him for what He can do for us rather than for who He is. The pagans went after idols for the same reason. Jesus was happy to provide food, but He wanted his friends to know He was more than a caterer!

Jesus used one of His most shocking metaphors to tell the crowd that they were seeking Him for too little. He was not only the sustenance of physical life, but also the source of eternal life. The metaphor was meant to shock them into looking beneath the surface of the miracle of the loaves and fishes.

Jesus warned them that His words were not literal (see John 6:63). If only they had stayed around long enough, they would have learned that Jesus used hard sayings to reveal the impure motives of some who tried to be close to Him. But they left the Bread of Heaven to find food that was more down to earth.

When Jesus tried to tell His followers that He was the real food, "the bread that came down from heaven" (John 6:58), the Jewish leaders on the fringe of the crowd were offended. They had fallen into the other great temptation of religious people: to serve God through merely human intellect, discipline, and tradition. This offended Jesus so much that He offended their understanding. He used a hard saying to conceal the key to life from the Jewish leaders.

The Lord hides His wisdom in the Holy Spirit so that the intellectually and religiously proud cannot find it through their natural talents. People committed to living by the power of their own intellects can't live with that offense to their minds.

The disciples were just as clueless, but they were not offended. They believed Jesus had a purpose in using the shocking language, and they stayed around to learn what He really meant.

To summarize: Symbolic language conceals truth from the proud, reveals profound truth to the humble, and jars us awake when we are tempted to use God rather than love Him. It also impacts our emotions—especially with dreams and visions, which are often symbolic rather than literal. Prosaic warnings may be ignored, but the symbols in dreams and visions may shake us out of our lethargy (see Job 33:15–18). The fact is, our feelings influence us greatly. Because they do, God uses pictures and symbols to connect with our feelings.

Interpreting Symbols

When Jesus mystified everyone with the invitation to drink His blood and eat His flesh, the twelve stayed close to Him and waited for Him to reveal His meaning. Today, we do this through prayer. In prayer, we draw close to Jesus, talk with Him, and wait on Him.

I'm now going to offer some practical suggestions for interpreting symbols, but none of the following advice comes close to the importance of prayer. Conversing with the One who gave us a symbol is the best way to discover its meaning.

Although it is possible to discern some consistent symbolic meanings in Scripture, as well as in contemporary experience, there is no "manual of symbols" for ready-made interpretations of the nonliteral elements in dreams and visions. Symbols have different meanings in different contexts. In one context, a baby may represent a new ministry. In another, a baby may represent immaturity. Pay close attention to the context. Search both Scripture and contemporary experience for the possible meaning of symbols. Invite God's Spirit to lead you.

Many things in the Bible have commonly understood symbolic meanings. For example, purple often stands for royalty. Vipers may represent either religious poison or gossip. Wine can represent joy. Wind may represent the Holy Spirit, or it may symbolize judgment (see John 3:8; 1 Kings 19:11).

Yet almost anything can have a nonliteral meaning. How do we discover these possibilities? Start by using a concordance. Find all of a word's occurrences. Read the context in which the word lies. The concordance usually reveals several possible symbolic meanings, but frequently while I am searching, one meaning seems to jump out at me, fitting perfectly into the context of my dream or vision.

Sometimes symbols are taken from our contemporary experience rather than from the Bible. When this happens, look for commonplace associations. What do you usually associate with the symbol? For example, a dream of an airplane crashing because of pilot error might mean the airplane represents a ministry taking you to spiritual heights, but because of the leaders' inexperience, the ministry is headed for a major disaster. It could be a warning to pray for the ministry's leaders. Our thoughts and feelings about the symbol are important too, for God chooses symbols that uniquely communicate with us.

Another practical tip for understanding dreams or visions is to pay attention to any detail that stands out. That detail may be a major clue to the meaning of the revelation. But don't try to get a meaning out of every detail. The context of the dream or vision will determine which details are relevant.

Over the years, as you treasure the dreams and visions the Lord gives you, you may find that you have acquired your own personalized dream vocabulary. But again, none of the above guidance for interpreting symbols is any substitute for *prayer*.

Remember that God gives us these dreams, visions, and words to prompt us to pray. Our goal is to build up the Body of Christ, and whatever He reveals is first and foremost a matter for prayer.

When we want to understand a divine communication, whether a scriptural text or a dream, we should pray, consult others who have wisdom in this area, and make use of any scholarly resource at our disposal. But we want our ultimate confidence to be in God to make His revelations clear, rather than in our intellectual capacities.

I have spent this time on symbolic meanings because a common mistake made in interpreting dreams and visions is to take something literally that was intended to be taken symbolically. There are no rigid rules to automatically decipher symbols. *Discernment is acquired in prayer over time and with practice.*

Another bit of advice: Most of the time, negative events in dreams and visions are warnings, not decreed events (see Job 33:13–18). A dream may warn us what will happen if we do not repent of a certain attitude or behavior. Every dream is an encouragement to pray.

Tormenting Dreams

In her dream, she was being shot repeatedly with a machine gun and felt every bullet, but she could not fall. The force of the shots held up her body. She could not die, so the bullets just kept tearing into her.

This was one dream my wife Leesa woke up to shortly after she began to have prophetic dreams. All prophetic people I know are subject to tormenting dreams.

Sometimes the devil is the source of these dreams. He is a master deceiver and will imitate the ways that God speaks (see chapter 8 for more on this). But we ourselves can be the source of a tormenting dream. If we fall asleep worrying, chances are we will have a negative dream about our worries. Movies we watch (especially horror movies), alcohol, certain kinds of foods, and some kinds of drugs (legal as well as illegal) can also affect our dreams.

How can we tell the difference between a true warning dream and a tormenting dream?

- First, consider any connection between the dream and what we were doing just before we fell asleep.
- Second, does the dream reflect something we habitually fear or worry about? Here is a point of prayer! Fear and worry are entry points for demonic deception.
- Third, does the dream destroy hope or make us feel that neither prayer nor repentance will help? Hopelessness and condemnation are signs of the accuser.

If we consistently ask the Lord to show us the difference between His dreams and those of our flesh or from the enemy, we will learn to discern the source.

When Leesa first began to have prophetic dreams, she often had a tormenting one. But when we began to pray every night before bed, asking God to keep the devil from invading her dreams, the invasions stopped. She was still visited by a tormenting dream sometimes, but that is part of being prophetic.

Prophets do not live in a tidy world. Confusion and ambiguity are their frequent companions. A fleeting vision or a barely remembered dream may hold the key for someone's rescue. Of all the gifts, none seem to rest on such flimsy experiences as prophecy. No ministry is as difficult to learn. It may also be the most valuable of all the gifts. It is the only spiritual gift that the apostle Paul singled out and urged the whole Church to pursue (see 1 Corinthians 14:1, 39).

Be patient with yourself as you learn to understand the prophetic language of the Holy Spirit. Humble persistence is more important than intelligence when discovering what only God can reveal. Pray, and pray some more. Understanding is the reward for those "who because of practice have their senses trained to distinguish between good and evil" (Hebrews 5:14 NASB).

SIX

Avoiding Prophetic Craziness

Not all crazy people are in asylums—and some are running around imitating prophets! They get away with it because some real prophets seem barely sane.

I'm not just talking about today's genuine prophets. I also mean the prophets of the Bible. If Jeremiah were ministering today, churchgoing people would recommend Prozac and counseling. Hosea married a prostitute—one who had other men's babies. Isaiah went around naked for three years. What would we do with these folks if they were in our congregation?

The bizarre behavior of the biblical prophets is now safely tucked away in the pages of the Bible. And for many churchgoers, the Bible is the most unread book, so many are not aware of the strange things in it. There is also a theological reason why we are not troubled by the biblical prophets' conduct: In historic hindsight, God stands behind their weird ways.

God is the one who told Jeremiah, Hosea, Isaiah, and others to do peculiar things. But that should *not* make us comfortable with

God. The only way to derive comfort here is to assume that God does not speak anymore except in the pages of the Bible, or that He has given up His strange ways. But you probably would not be reading this book if you believed that! It is much more likely that you believe God still speaks today and that He might ask even you to do something strange. Staying humble, wise, and careful will keep you out of trouble.

Prophetic Megalomania

When I first began pursuing prophetic ministry, I met a young man I will call Robert. Walking along the sidewalk after a rain, he noticed a dead worm. He thought God was speaking to him about the worm. So he picked it up, expecting that if he prayed for it, God would bring it back to life. The worm did not respond. Undaunted, he decided God was leading him to put the worm into an envelope and give it to a leader of a prominent Christian movement. Robert had no idea why God wanted him to do this. He also had no authority or place within the movement.

When he walked into the offices of the ministry to deliver the deceased worm, he was not given a warm reception. He took this to mean that those serving the leader were jealous and afraid that Robert might become closer to the leader than they were. But when the leader opened the envelope, he gave the worm immediate burial in the wastebasket, thanked Robert, and told him goodbye.

Now, Robert was sure that his failure to worm his way into the movement was due to the corrupt hearts of the underlings who had allowed an evil spirit access to the ministry offices. He could not accept that his strange act had anything to do with his rejection.

I followed this young man's career for a while longer, and instead of learning from the failures of his bizarre behavior, Robert developed a theology to justify it. God supposedly "told" him that his ministry would be rejected. Armed with the weird incidents of the Bible and a supposed divine promise of rejection, he could blame someone else for his failures. I know of at least one whole church he turned off to the gifts of the Spirit, thus helping them to despise the gift of prophecy in particular.

This is tragic, because Robert is not a prophet. Several leaders tried to help him see this, but they were not able to reach him. In the book of Proverbs, the fool is depicted as a megalomaniac beyond correction (see Proverbs 27:22). If we are foolish enough, we will always be able to find something in the Bible to justify or excuse wrong or weird behavior or corruption in our hearts.

Thankfully, I have met only one or two people in the prophetic ministry like Robert. But his example reminds us that before we use the Bible's prophets to justify some action, we should remember that God commanded them to do these things. The issue was not discerning accurately; the issue was obedience. We should also expect God's voice to be very clear before we do something strange, especially when it could hurt someone. So, the first line is *always* prayer—pray! Ask for confirmation. Pray! Ask for wisdom and gentleness. Pray!

Still, sometimes the Lord does do things that appear unorthodox or strange. But there is a right way and a wrong way to respond to these acts.

Don't Glorify the Strange

Sometimes the Spirit picked people up physically and dropped them off at other locations (see 1 Kings 18:12; Acts 8:39). God caused a donkey to speak (see Numbers 22:21–30). These things happened, and God did them.

Why? Sometimes He did some strange act to offend the minds of the religious know-it-alls, sometimes to frustrate the self-satisfaction of the proud, and sometimes for other reasons He has never shared. The point is that from beginning to end in the Bible, God did things that seem strange to us. Why would we imagine that once the Bible was completed, God would change His ways to accommodate our sense of good taste?

How, then, should we respond when we encounter one of God's strange acts today? We should glorify *Him* for the experience. Unfortunately, some in the Church glorify the *experience*. Once I was in a meeting that was part of a series where God had been revealing His presence with unusual physical manifestations. Five people gave testimonies about this at the start of the meeting. The first four told about life-changing encounters with God and included humorous details of the physical phenomena. The fifth told how her life had been changed, but said that she had not experienced any physical manifestations.

The interviewer said to the crowd, "See, that shows you don't have to shake or fall down to experience the power of God." Then as a group prayed on the stage for that fifth person, he added, "But God's gonna get you yet." The crowd erupted into laughter and applause, hoping she would fall or shake. She didn't.

The interviewer's last statement told the crowd that if you have not shaken, you have not really met God's power. He was *glorifying the manifestations of God's presence rather than God*. When we do this, we are like children on Christmas morning who unwrap valuable gifts but play instead with the shiny wrapping paper. When God gives physical manifestations, they are just the wrapping paper around His presence. *His presence is the real gift!* His presence is crucial, not how the presence is manifested.

Putting our focus on manifestations and methods always leads us into deception. We must keep our eyes on the One who is truth. That is why humility is so important. Humble people are less easily deceived, and even when they are deceived, they are more quickly corrected.

Reproducing the Strange

Trying to reproduce the strange can be just as damaging as glorifying the strange. Often the strange happening is a singular, sovereign event. Consider the handkerchiefs taken from Paul's body.

The Bible only tells about this once, in Ephesus, where people used all sorts of charms to manipulate spirits and the forces of nature. Christians (some sincere and some not) try to reproduce this today by blessing prayer cloths and giving (or selling) them to the sick.

I'm not saying that God has not healed the sick today using this method (or even stranger ones). But those passing out prayer cloths are not getting the same results as Paul did. Instead of copying the *character* of the apostle Paul, they copy a *method*. When we get to the point where we do all things for the sake of the Gospel and suffer for Christ as Paul did (see 1 Corinthians 9:23; 2 Corinthians 11:16–32), maybe God will imbue our clothing with a little power. But it is a lot easier to pass out prayer cloths than to imitate Paul's character.

One more thing to notice: Paul talked a lot more about *the Lord* than he did about his strange experiences with the Lord. He never even mentioned the handkerchief episode; his friend Luke told that story. Luke's point was not to introduce a new healing method, but to show the superior power of Jesus Christ over magic.

Still, at times God still does strange things. He may do something both strange and *new*—and He may ask *us* to do something strange and new. What will our response be?

False Guilt

A lady presented me with the following problem: She had been praying for a blind lady to receive her sight. Nothing happened. The thought of the time Jesus spit on the ground and put mud on a blind man's eyes came to her. She felt that if she would do the same, the blind lady would be healed. But they were standing on a carpeted floor; there was no dirt nearby. And she was afraid of doing something so weird—yet Jesus had done it. She felt guilty for her fear. And the guiltier she felt, the more she felt He was leading her to do it. But was He? Was her hesitation due to her fear of looking foolish, or to uncertainty about the leading? In the end, she didn't spit, and the blind lady didn't see. Now she was tormented with guilt for not applying the mud. This had happened in a foreign country, making it impractical for her to go back and pray again for the blind person using the mud method.

This lady asked me, "What should I have done? Was the impulse to make mud with my saliva from the Lord or from myself?"

I told her that I didn't think it was from the Lord. Here's why: First, it is natural for us to think of biblical passages that correspond to our prayers. When I pray for deaf people, I often wonder if I should put my fingers in their ears, something Jesus did (see Mark 7:32–33).

Second, when we are praying unsuccessfully for a miracle, we naturally search for a reason. We may think we are not following the Bible literally enough or don't have enough faith or that there is sin in our life.

Third, the lady did not have certainty or peace about doing this. She was more worried about missing God's leading than she was about obeying God. She would have been happy to obey if she really knew it was God leading her. Remember that when God commanded the prophets of the Bible to do something weird, He did it *so clearly* that they did not wonder whether the command came from Him or from their emotions.

Fourth, this lady was relatively new at hearing God's voice. She was contemplating a prophetic act beyond her level of faith (see Romans 12:6). These factors persuaded me to conclude that her emotions had been leading her to apply the mud, not God.

She could have asked God to confirm to her that the leading was from Him. She could have included the blind lady by saying, "You'll probably think this is crazy, and I don't blame you, but I feel like doing what Jesus did—making mud with my saliva and putting it on your eyes. What do you think?"

The blind lady might have said, "No way!" Or she might have said, "Well, what have I got to lose? My eyes are no good to me now anyway. Give it a try."

In this way, this ministering lady would have been treating the blind lady as a *person*, a beloved image bearer of God, and not an *experiment*.

Training for the Prophetic

Have you ever gone to church on Sunday morning and heard the leaders say, "Who will give the sermon this morning?" Why not? Because everyone knows the craziness that would bring into the church. Yet some churches practice prophecy this way, taking a programmed pause during which anyone may "prophesy."

I have watched churches try to do prophetic ministry in this way and have never seen it build a strong prophetic ministry. This method can make people ignore—or even despise—prophetic ministry. Why?

We set a high standard for the one who teaches us on Sunday morning—a certain level of character and ability. Why not set the same standards for those who prophesy to the whole church? Raise the bar instead of lowering it. Paul suggests this when he limits the number of prophets to two or three who may speak in the meetings (see 1 Corinthians 14:29).

Someone might object that letting only mature prophets address the whole church quenches the Spirit (see 1 Thessalonians 5:19). But we are trying to ensure that what is said really does come from the Spirit. I'm not saying that God would never give a word to the whole church through an inexperienced prophet. Anyone who thinks he or she has a revelation for the whole church is always free to ask an elder for permission to speak. If the elder thinks it is appropriate, he or she may allow the person to speak, or one of those leading the service may give the word.

Paul's comments in 1 Corinthians 14 lead us to believe that the gift of prophecy should be widely distributed in the Church. He tells us to pursue spiritual gifts, especially prophecy (see verse 1). Furthermore, Peter says that prophetic experiences should be normal for the Church (see Acts 2:17–21). James leads us to believe that the gift of teaching will be much rarer than the gift of prophecy when he says, "Not many of you should presume to be teachers . . ." (James 3:1). In my church, we have many more prophets than teachers.

How do people learn to prophesy if only a few can address the whole church on a Sunday morning? They learn best in home groups, training classes, seminars, and other small groups. After being trained, they can serve on ministry teams that pray over people after services. And don't despise a "nonpublic" word. Some of the most wonderful prophetic words I've received have been given in an informal way.

Ten Rules for Prophetic Success

If we obey the following ten rules, we may avoid some unnecessary trouble.

Rule 1: Emphasize the main and the plain, not the rare and the bizarre. Do this in your Scripture study and in your prophetic ministry.

Rule 2: Don't do anything strange without a *clear* leading from God.

Rule 3: Don't do anything prophetically that is potentially embarrassing or harmful to another person, without his or her permission. You are ministering to God's children, not rebellious idolaters. That is a big difference. Also remember that you are not Elijah. When you get to his level of commitment and skill, you can have a little more latitude with rule 3.

Rule 4: Repeat after me: "I am not an exception to the rules. I am a beginner in the school of the prophets."

Rules 5 through 10: See rule 4.

Strive to be as normal and unreligious as possible if you want your message to be received. That was Paul's advice (see 1 Corinthians 14:23–25). Do things decently and in order, for God is a God of peace (see 1 Corinthians 14:33, 40). If He wants to violate the peace, fine. But we should work to keep it.

The next chapter offers some guidelines not only for keeping the peace, but also for obtaining the maximum benefit from our prophetic words.

SEVEN

Giving Prophetic Messages

The word *dreams* flashed into my mind as I looked at a lady in the third row. That was it, just the word *dreams*. I felt that I was supposed to speak to the lady, but the word was just too general. I felt the need to improve it. In front of everyone, I asked her if she had been praying to have dreams. In front of everyone, she said no!

A few minutes later, she raised her hand and told us that she had recently read one of my books and was now having vivid dreams. She had no one to talk to about what was happening, and had asked God to let us meet. She didn't know I was coming to her city and found out about the meeting just in time to attend.

This was a divine appointment. The Lord had even given me the subject of our meeting: her dreams. I almost spoiled it by trying to improve it. I should have simply said to her, "When I looked at you, the word *dreams* flashed into my mind. Does that mean anything to you?" Resist the temptation to add to what the Lord gives you.

Realizing the Power of Obedience

I failed to appreciate the power of the word I had been given and thought I could improve it by making it more specific. I was *adding to* the revelation I had received. Sometimes, we are tempted to add a few specific details to make us appear more powerful. But *don't do it*. If the word is from the Lord, it will have power.

Leprosy. The word popped into my mind out of nowhere. I was seated at a conference table with twenty Christians—some church leaders, but some in business, entertainment, and media. We had decided to close the meeting by praying for one another when *leprosy* captured my attention. I asked the Lord what it meant and to whom it applied, but got no answer.

I was sure that the word was from the Lord. Two men from Israel sat at the table, and my best guess was that it applied to one of them. I thought about asking them, but I felt a hesitation to do so.

After about ten minutes, I asked the group, "Does *leprosy* mean anything to anyone here?"

No one said anything for a minute. Then a banker and investor spoke up. He said that he had recently invested in a leper colony in India. Compassion had moved him to make the investment that gave a business to a leper colony of over seven hundred people. We prayed over the businessman about his investment and some other things in his life.

Later I had dinner with him, and he told me how powerful the whole experience was for him. The single word *leprosy* and the prayer following confirmed a direction he was taking in his business and let him know that the Lord was pleased with him. I'm glad I did not add to the word! Words from the Lord are powerful even when they simple or single. Our job is to obey and speak, even if we don't know to whom they apply.

Observing the Golden Rule

Those who want to look like "great prophets" always end up needlessly hurting others. Real prophets not only see our secrets, but also are full of mercy. God uses kindness to lead us to repentance, and they follow His example (see Romans 2:4).

Truly great prophets treat people as they want to be treated (see Luke 6:31). When they have a word for someone, they ask God not only for the way in which to deliver the message, but the timing of its delivery as well.

If someone saw a sin in your life, how would you want him or her to call it out? Would you want that person to tell everyone what he or she had seen about you? That might make the individual look like a powerful prophet to some, but what would it do to you?

The greatest Prophet once said, "Bless those who curse you" (Luke 6:28). The few who will give that kind of blessing are entrusted with the greatest of God's secrets, for God knows that they won't use His secrets for cruelty, but rather as His tools of mercy and love for reshaping damaged lives.

Trusting God's Timing

When we have a real revelation with the right interpretation, we may still deliver the message without anyone benefiting—because we give it at the wrong time. A wise prophet knows that "like apples of gold in settings of silver, is a word spoken at the proper time" (Proverbs 25:11 NASB). Such a timely word is a work of art that brings both joy to the speaker and blessing to the hearer (see Proverbs 15:23).

Whatever is revealed to you, *pray first*. Never give a prophetic word to someone without asking and receiving *the Lord's permission*. I am often asked, "How do we know if we have the Lord's permission to give the word?" The answer is, "He will tell us, if we ask Him."

Why would God give us a revelation and not tell us how to use it? If we had the capacity to receive the revelation, we also have the capacity to hear what to do with it. We also need to ask the Lord to show us how to apply the revelation, just as much as we need Him to give us the revelation and its interpretation. People are different; the same truth may need to be applied in different ways to different hearers. *The Holy Spirit must illumine each step of the process if we are ever to be a blessing to anyone.*

Sometimes the Lord does not give a prophet an interpretation or application of a revelation, but He still has him or her speak the revelation. We must be careful not to say more than God has said. If we add anything, we should make it clear which part was the revelation and which part was our own opinion regarding its meaning and application. Our opinion may be valuable, but if we are not carefully obedient, we can lead our hearers to believe that our opinion is what God has said—and that is dangerously deceptive.

Being Kind

The Lord's kindness is the standard for all prophetic ministry. Remember, the purpose of this ministry is to build up the Body of Christ. When we give people words from the Lord, we should make them feel at ease. Always give prophetic words with tenderness and humility. People should feel the Lord's kindness and love through us.

Old Testament prophets frequently spoke angry words from God. These words were spoken to a rebellious people given to idolatry or hypocrisy. But angry, self-righteous, judgmental, and accusatory messages rarely do any good. Jesus reserved His angry words for self-righteous, hypocritical, religious leaders (see Matthew 23). If God has an angry message for the Church today, I expect it would come from a humble, broken-hearted prophet who loves the Church and identifies with its sin, and who moves at the highest level of revelation (see Daniel 9:4–19). Most angry "prophetic" words I hear usually flow from a stream of unhealed anger in the prophet. Give every message with gentleness and tact.

All prophets (and all believers) would do well to ask the Holy Spirit to write the following words on their hearts:

> A gentle answer turns away wrath, but a harsh word stirs up anger (Proverbs 15:1).

> Through patience a ruler can be persuaded, and a gentle tongue can break a bone (Proverbs 25:15).

If we frame our messages tactfully and avoid attacks on a person's character, our words are more likely to be received in the hearts of our hearers.

Interceding

In the center of heaven are hundreds of millions of angels. Among the angels are twenty-four thrones with twenty-four elders, and four living creatures flying around a single throne encircled by an emerald rainbow. In the very center of heaven sits the Lord Jesus Christ. The whole heavenly entourage gazes on the beauty of that glorious Person and sings His praises nonstop (see Revelation 4–5).

But what is *Jesus* doing? He labors in prayer for you and for me, and for all those He is drawing to His Father (see Hebrews 7:25). The greatest Prophet is also the greatest Priest, and though He is all-knowing and all-powerful, He is still praying!

Following the Spirit of Jesus, great prophets have always been great interceders. If we truly want our prophetic word to draw our hearers to God, then we should pray for them when we receive the revelation, while we are giving it, and after we deliver it.

Intercession is hard work; it is easier to do almost *anything* other than pray. But it may be that our prayers, not our message, are what the Lord uses to help a person. After Isaiah delivered one of his most difficult messages, he said, "I will wait for the LORD, who is hiding his face from the descendants of Jacob. I will put my trust in him" (Isaiah 8:17). Follow Isaiah's example. Pray. Wait for the Lord. Put your trust in Him.

Withholding Words

Daniel was not only a prophet; he was a wise prophet (see Ezekiel 28:3). When he received one of his most troubling visions, he kept it to himself (see Daniel 7:28). He did not get upset when God gave him a vision and refused to let him share it. He did not need to prove that he was a spectacular prophet by sharing the vision. He knew the reward of living in obedience to the Lord.

The discipline to be silent when God is silent, or when He has withheld permission to speak, shows prophetic maturity. God does not reveal His secrets to blabbermouths, but to those who fear Him (see Psalm 25:14). No one gets to the highest level of prophetic ministry without prophetic restraint. These are the prophets who can be trusted with a revelation not yet ripe for sharing, that must be "sealed" for a later use (see Isaiah 8:16; 29:11; Daniel 8:26; 12:4, 9). These trusted friends of God have *His* interests at heart.

Why would God show a prophet something and not give him or her permission to share it? Perhaps He is calling the prophet to intercede instead of prophesy. In fact, *unless the Lord says otherwise, every revelation is also a call to prayer.* Maybe the timing for the message is not yet right. Sometimes the Lord gives a message in stages, and the prophet who speaks a partial message as if it were the whole message may lead someone astray.

It is also possible that we may see accurately what someone is planning to do, but not what God wants that person to do. If we speak without God's permission, we may confirm man's plans rather than God's. In that case, we will have become part of the deception instead of part of the deliverance.

Saying "Thus Says the Lord"

Should you introduce your prophetic message by saying "thus says the Lord"? Old Testament prophets frequently did. The New Testament counterpart is "the Holy Spirit says" (Acts 21:11). When the prophets used this phrase, they were claiming to speak the precise words of God, not their interpretations or applications of the revelation they had received. "Thus says the Lord" allowed no debate. It meant, "This is exactly what God has said." These were not words of personal prophecy, but God's words over nations. These prophets had proven character and experience. We should be quick to imitate their passion for God and slow to imitate their vocabulary.

When we say "thus says the Lord" to someone, he or she may feel controlled or manipulated because it is intuitively obvious that we don't have the same authority as the biblical prophets who spoke over nations. I am not saying that it is always wrong to say this, only that most of those using it do not have the authority to use it. The prophets I know who have the most authority rarely use the phrase.

On the other hand, I know good prophets who use the phrase constantly when they prophesy. We each need to obey the Lord, not compare ourselves with others.

Grandiose Prophecies

I have noticed that among some gifted prophets, prophetic words are often given in grandiose terms. I heard a prophet tell a lady that God would use her "to change nations." Perhaps this was so, since anyone who prays regularly for nations may play a part in

Biblical Prophecy

changing them. But I don't think that is the way the lady or that church received the word. "Change the nations" calls to mind the apostle Paul, not a patient prayer warrior.

Overusing grandiose language produces sickness in the Church for these reasons:

- After a while, when we see these words falling to the ground, we may start ignoring prophetic words—or despising them.
- Inflated words can have an inflating effect on the person who receives them (as you will see in the story that begins chapter 8).
- When we tell people that they are going to do something incredible or that they have incredible character, we may make them believe that their significance lies in their performance or character. This gives the devil's accusing ministry great success (see Revelation 12:10). In truth, we are significant only because an infinite, perfect Person loves us!

According to Paul, our stability comes from experiencing God's infinite love (see Ephesians 3:14–21). Remember that "the testimony of Jesus is the spirit of prophecy" (Revelation 19:10 NASB). Therefore, all our prophetic words need to direct people to *His* greatness, not our greatness. Worship belongs to Him, not to the one who gave the word, nor even to the word itself. Become a humble messenger!

Authority Subject to Scripture

Prophetic words are always subject to the authority of Scripture. In the Old Testament, even if a prophetic word came true and was confirmed by miraculous signs, it was not to be followed if it contradicted the teaching of Scripture (God's commands; see Deuteronomy 13:1–5). During Isaiah's time, people often consulted mediums. Isaiah set forth a standard to distinguish true prophets: "To the Law and to the testimony! If they do not speak in accordance with this word, it is because they have no dawn" (Isaiah 8:20 NASB).

Paul addressed the same problem in Corinth, where some claimed that they were led to ignore his teaching due to their own prophetic inspiration. He wrote, "If anyone thinks they are a prophet or otherwise gifted by the Spirit, let them acknowledge that what I am writing to you is the Lord's command" (1 Corinthians 14:37). The authority of Scripture is universal, for all people, always. Personal revelation, on the other hand, is only for the people to whom it is given, for that time.

How much weight should we give to personal prophetic words? Jeremiah certainly expected the people to base their decision on *his* prophetic word. When the people asked him whether they should stay in Judah or flee to Egypt, he said the Lord would only protect them if they stayed in Judah (see Jeremiah 42). The people did not listen, and most of them died in Egypt. But we do not use Jeremiah or any Old Testament prophet as our model for the authority of today's personal prophetic words.

It is an error to use corporate examples as a model for personal words. In a corporate word, the prophet represented the voice of God to a nation that acknowledged Him as their only ruler. In the above example, Jeremiah was not speaking to individuals to give them some guidance about where they should live; he was speaking to the remnant of the rebellious nation, telling them how God would allow their survival.

God used prophets to say things that neither the king nor the nation wanted to believe. To help the people believe, He established the prophets' authority. He came down in a cloud to speak with Moses in front of all the people (see Exodus 19:9). He caused the waters of the Jordan to stand up so that the people would follow Joshua (see Joshua 3:7–17). He gave extraordinary accuracy to Samuel so that none of his words fell to the ground (see 1 Samuel 3:19). He confirmed Elijah's words by withholding rain and by sending fire from heaven (see 1 Kings 17:1; 18:36–38). The Old Testament prophets were thus verified.

When Jesus came, He gave this authority to the apostles, not to the prophets. The authority structure of the Church differs from that of Israel. Apostles, not prophets, have trans-local authority in the Body of Christ. New Testament apostles gave corporate words to the whole Church. God revealed to each apostle where his sphere of authority lay, and the Church recognized that authority. New Testament prophets had a much greater ministry in personal rather than corporate words. They spoke to individuals for their comfort, encouragement, and strengthening (see Acts 15:32; 1 Corinthians 14:3). They also gave corporate words (see Acts 11:27–30), but the New Testament emphasizes ministry to individuals.

On the local level, the elders of individual churches, not prophets, have authority. Most New Testament prophets are not elders or leaders. Paul wrote that it is "the elders who direct the affairs of the church" (1 Timothy 5:17). And here is a critical point: *All New Testament authority is given to direct the affairs of the Church, not people's personal lives.* When the leaders of a church or a Christian movement start to exert authority over the personal lives of their followers, they are on the road that leads to becoming a cult. Neither prophets nor pastors should be making our personal decisions for us.

Jesus brought us into a more intimate relationship with the Father than the saints of the Old Testament experienced. The normal experience for us is to hear His voice (see John 10:4). We have the Holy Spirit to lead us (see Romans 8:14). The Father expects us to hear from the Spirit regarding our personal decisions. This does not mean that prophets cannot help. They can support, confirm, or clarify what we believe the Lord is saying to us. They can cause us to pray about directions we had not considered. But they should never cause us to give up our privilege of hearing God's voice for ourselves. God will never allow us to excuse our bad decisions by saying, "It was that prophet You gave me!"

This does not mean that New Testament prophets do not speak authoritative words. In fact, at the end of the age, in a prophetic revival, the two most powerful prophets' authority will be established like that of the prophets of old (see Revelation 11:3–12).

Respecting Pastoral Authority

I met a young man who was kind, sincere, and prophetically gifted. He felt the Lord had shown him how to improve his church. He told the pastor that he should shut the church down for a month so that they could all really learn how to do church. He could not understand why the pastor rejected his word!

I have no doubt that the young man saw some wrong patterns in his church, but he did not respect the authority of his pastor. This undermined the effectiveness of any message he might have heard from the Lord.

Here are a couple of important ways to show respect for pastoral authority:

- Don't give a major correction without tact. The young man did not realize that he was saying that his pastor's entire previous ministry at that church was flawed. It was wrong to approach someone like this, who had been given authority to direct the affairs of the church and authority to watch over that young man's soul (see 1 Timothy 5:17; Hebrews 13:17).
- Don't give a message you have no authority to give. Words such as a message of radical redirection for a ministry are usually entrusted to a prophet with experience and acknowledged divine authority. This beginner prophet was a businessman who had never received any prophetic training. I asked how he would like it if someone with no business experience told him to shut down his business for

a month so that he could really learn how to do business. He got the picture, but the damage already had been done.

The purpose of divine authority is different from earthly authority. It is given to lead people into a deeper intimacy with Jesus, not to control them. Unlike earthly authority, *divine authority eludes those who seek it, leaves those who abuse it, and rests on those who rest in the Word.*

EIGHT

Deceptions, Demons, and False Prophets

Twelve of us were sitting in a circle. Most of us were pastors. Only one was a prophet. He prophesied over three of us in succession with perfect accuracy about our past and present, and then told us about our future. We were amazed. How could this guy know the secrets of our hearts without ever having met us? We believed him.

Turning to a fourth pastor, he said that in the last days the believing Church in America would be divided into twelve powerful tribes. Looking straight at the pastor, he said, "And you are going to lead one of these twelve tribes."

I should have known immediately that this was wrong. Not because the pastor had a small church. Not because he did not exhibit any gifts of the Holy Spirit. And not because he lacked the relational skills to lead great numbers—but because when he heard the prophecy, he smiled a welcoming smile. If he had possessed a heart for that calling, he would have trembled.

The prophecy had immediate destructive effects in the pastor's life. It made him think more highly of himself than he should have.

A year later, that pastor asked the prophet why he thought things were plummeting in his life. To his credit, the prophet told the pastor he had been wrong in his prophecy: "I'm laying down the prophecies I gave about movements last year."

Why would a pastor believe a wrong prophecy about himself? As I got to know this pastor, I began to see God's greater purpose in his life. I believe that buried in his soul was a lie of the enemy that he would find significance in this life only by becoming *recognized* as a great leader by the Church. The "wrong" prophecy had agreed with the lie he already believed, which then moved right into his heart.

How could such a gifted prophet miss it so badly? Or was God revealing the pastor's heart to himself through this "miss"? Did this error mean the prophet was a false prophet? Before we can answer that, let's talk about counterfeit ministry.

Counterfeit Ministry

The devil cannot create. Only God can create. Therefore, one of the devil's main strategies is to try to counterfeit what God does. Does the Lord speak to His people and lead them? The devil will try! Does the Lord give wisdom to His people? The devil has his own "wisdom," which he attempts to impart to the Church (see James 3:15). Does the Holy Spirit speak to us about our sin and convict us (see John 16:8)? The devil speaks, too. But instead of bringing conviction leading to hope, he accuses and leads to despair (see Revelation 12:10).

The devil has false messiahs and false apostles whom he empowers to do counterfeit signs, wonders, and miracles (see Matthew 24:24; 2 Corinthians 11:13–15; 2 Thessalonians 2:9; Revelation 16:14). He has false prophets to whom he may impart a "lying spirit" to deceive a king (see 1 Kings 22:21), or through whom he may impart a "spirit of divination" to predict the future with some degree of accuracy (see Acts 16:16). He can provide a counterfeit anointing (see 1 John 2:27) that provides false teachers and false elders with false humility, false knowledge, and false doctrines (see Acts 20:29–31; Colossians 2:18, 23; 1 Timothy 6:3–5; 2 Peter 2:1–3, 20).

These teachers and elders "abandon the faith and follow deceiving spirits and things taught by demons" (1 Timothy 4:1). In this way, the devil can introduce demonic doctrines into the Church. The devil also sends false brothers into the Church to steal the children's bread and betray its leaders (see 2 Corinthians 11:26). The devil will attempt to counterfeit everything God does, even the gifts God has given to the Church.

Why does Satan want to substitute false ministry for the real ministry of the Holy Spirit?

- Many religious people would never knowingly follow evil. Satan therefore produces an appealing counterfeit that leads the religious away from the truth, while they think they are serving God. Usually, they think the true worshipers are the ones who are deceived.
- Infiltrating the Church with false ministers and doctrines causes division that weakens the purity and power of the Church.
- Counterfeit ministers empowered with false gifts make the Church afraid of *real* supernatural gifts and those who use them. The enemy has been so successful with this that part of the Church now has more confidence in Satan's ability to deceive them than in Jesus' ability to lead them!

False Prophets

Here are some things to be aware of that false prophets can and will do:

- Predict the future and perform wonders (see Jeremiah 23:10; Isaiah 44:25; Matthew 7:21–23; 24:24)

- Seek to undermine true prophets. When an opening comes, false prophets persecute those who are true (see Jeremiah 23:1–17; 1 John 4:6)
- Tell people that wonderful things are coming, when true prophets have decreed judgment instead (see Jeremiah 23)
- Live in and promote immorality among God's people (see Jeremiah 23:14; Revelation 2:14, 20–23)
- Deny basic truths of the faith (see 2 Peter 2:1–3)
- Use their power to lead people away from the true God to false gods (see Deuteronomy 13:1–5; Jeremiah 23:13; Acts 13:6–8)

A false prophet is not a prophet who makes a mistake in a prediction. Deuteronomy 18:15–22 is used by some to teach that if a prophet made a mistake, he was stoned. But the text from this passage is not about prophets in general. In verse 15, Moses predicts, "The LORD your God will raise up for you a prophet like me from among you, from your fellow Israelites." The key to understanding the prophecy is the phrase *like me.* Moses was unique among all the prophets in the following ways (see also Numbers 12:6–8; Deuteronomy 34:10–12):

- Moses mediated the Old Covenant. He stood between the people and God, representing both. When he told the Israelites that God would give them "a prophet like me," he was referring to the Messiah, and this is exactly how the New Testament believers understood the prophecy (see Acts 3:17–26; 7:37).
- The false prophet of Deuteronomy 18:20 was to be put to death not because he made a mistake, but because he presumed to be like Moses while attempting to lead the people to other gods.

- No other text in the Old Testament supports the idea that a prophet was executed for a mistake, and there is no example of the people ever applying Deuteronomy 18:15–22 in this way. Note that when Nathan made a mistake by speaking in the name of the Lord to David, telling him to go ahead with his plans to build the Temple, God simply corrected Nathan. No one called him a false prophet or attempted to stone him (see 2 Samuel 7:1–17).

Jesus said that we recognize false prophets by the fruit of their ministry, not by their power, miracles, or accuracy (see Matthew 7:15–23). And if New Testament prophets could not make mistakes, why did Paul command the Church to judge prophetic words (see 1 Corinthians 14:29)?

All teachers, pastors, and evangelists make mistakes. Even the apostle Peter made such a serious mistake that Paul had to rebuke him publicly (see Galatians 2:11–21). Why can't we show prophets the same mercy? Why should prophetic ministry be the only ministry that is not allowed a single mistake, and prophets the only ones not allowed to grow in grace?

New Testament Categories of Prophets

In the Old Testament, the average prophet was found in the schools of anonymous prophets. In the New Testament, the gift of prophecy is given to ordinary believers. The life and ministry of Jesus should be our goal. Two of my goals are to love Jesus like the apostle John and to teach like the apostle Paul. I am a long way from both, and I may never even get close to fulfilling them. That does not mean that the love I do have for Jesus is not real, or that my gift of teaching is counterfeit.

When we evaluate New Testament prophets, let's think in New Testament terms. For example, in 1 Corinthians 3:3 Paul described some Christians as "spiritual" and others as "carnal" (KJV), "fleshly"

(NASB), or "worldly" (NIV). Spiritual believers are those who so consistently walk with Christ that their lives reflect the fruit of the Spirit (see Galatians 5:22–23). The carnal believers, on the other hand, have had enough time to become spiritual, but remain immature because they have refused correction. They are better at blaming than repenting. There are also believers who are immature simply because they are young Christians who haven't had time to mature.

Let's think of prophets in these same categories. The spiritual prophet is mature in gifting and character. Then there is the immature but growing prophet, whose character and gifting are improving. There is also the carnal prophet who may be very gifted, but whose character deficiencies produce more strife than spiritual fruit. In terms of gifting, the immature prophet and the carnal prophet may look similar; it is only by the spiritual gift of discernment or by evaluating their ministries over time that we can distinguish between them.

Finally, there is the false prophet. This one has a supernatural gift but is not born again, and uses his or her gifting to lead people away from the Lord. Jesus warned that at the end of the age "many false prophets will appear and deceive many people" (Matthew 24:11), and that they will have extraordinary, supernatural power (see verse 24). So far, I have not encountered many false prophets *within* the Church. I find carnal prophets to be a much greater problem in the Church than false prophets. But as prophetic ministry becomes more established, we should expect to see more prophetic counterfeits. This will be a sign that the end of the age is drawing near.

Recognizing False Prophets

How do we recognize the counterfeit? Jude 4–19 is perhaps the best single passage that describes false ministers. At the top of Jude's list is that they "deny Jesus Christ" (verse 4). According to verse 11, their motives for ministry can be found in:

- "the way of Cain" (anger and rejection)
- "Balaam's error" (greed and immorality)
- "Korah's rebellion" (envy of God's anointed leaders)

False prophets' ministries are characterized by immorality, rejection of authority, selfishness, manipulation, grumbling, fault-finding, flattery, empty boasting, and the disappointment of all who trust them. They "do not have the Spirit" (verse 19). Jude's description fits not only false prophets, but also false apostles, teachers, and elders.

To identify the counterfeit with certainty, look for two things to occur in combination: First, counterfeit ministry denies the written Word of God. The denial doesn't involve a matter of interpretation, but rather a foundational doctrine of the Bible. Second, because the devil cannot produce the fruit of the Spirit, the false minister is devoid of spiritual life and fruit. You might think that fruitlessness and lifelessness make it easy to identify false prophets, but remember, false ministers are deceptive and winsome. Plus, they have a degree of power that seems to validate them. With that combination, they build a base of support before they reveal their true character. Jesus warned us that deceptive power would be so great in the last days that those who are false could "deceive, if possible, even the elect" (Matthew 24:24).

The best way to spot false anointing is with the discernment that comes from true anointing. We have been given the Holy Spirit "that we may understand what God has freely given us" (1 Corinthians 2:12) and that we may reject the counterfeit gifts of the devil. The Lord has given some in the Body the gift of "distinguishing between spirits" (1 Corinthians 12:10). They can discern the difference between the work of the Holy Spirit, demonic spirits, and human spirits.

So, we must conclude that the prophet at the beginning of this chapter who gave the mistaken prophecy was not a false prophet. He did not deny foundational doctrines and was not leading people away from God to other gods and into immorality. Still, how could he be so stunningly accurate with three people and miss it with the fourth?

Open Doors for Demonic Deception

Can an evil spirit deceive a true prophet? Let me list here some ways in which any believer can be influenced by demons. The Bible teaches that prolonged, voluntary sin in one of the following areas will give the devil a place of influence in our lives:

- Anger or unforgiveness (see Ephesians 4:26–27; 2 Corinthians 2:9–11)
- Lust, sexual immorality, or perversion (see 1 Corinthians 5:5)
- Hatred or violence (see Luke 9:54–56; John 8:44)
- Envy, jealousy, or selfish ambition (see James 3:13–18; 1 Samuel 18:8–11)
- Occult practices (see Leviticus 19:31; Deuteronomy 18:9–13; Acts 16:17–18)
- Idolatry or greed (see 1 Corinthians 10:20; Revelation 9:20; 1 Timothy 6:9; Colossians 3:5)
- Blasphemy (see 1 Timothy 1:20)

When prophetic people hold any of these within their hearts, demonic powers have a chance to distort their genuine revelatory insights or even give them a counterfeit revelation.

Was the prophet deceived by a demon when he gave the fourth pastor that wrong prophecy? I don't think so. There are other sources of deception. Our own hearts are also deceitful (see Jeremiah 17:9). We are prone to lie to ourselves. And remember, when we are trying to hear from God, we are always dealing with revelation, interpretation, and application. We may mistake our own thoughts for God's revelation, or we may have a true revelation and give it a wrong interpretation or application.

What contaminates this process? The Lord promises to give us the desires of our heart as we *delight in Him* (see Psalm 37:4). When we delight in something *other than Him*, Paul warns of the result: "Those who live according to the flesh have their minds set on what the flesh desires; but those who live in accordance with the Spirit have their minds set on what the Spirit desires" (Romans 8:5). The normal state of growing Christians is to set their minds on God, delighting in Him. But when we turn away, our desires deceive us (see Ephesians 4:22), corrupt us (see 2 Peter 1:4), and "choke the word, making it unfruitful" (Mark 4:19). A wrong desire can contaminate the process of discerning God's voice. That prophet's words may have been contaminated, but God may have used what he said to reveal to the pastor the lies he was believing!

Here are some desires that can contaminate the process:

- The desire for prominence. This desire can make it impossible to hear the voice of God (see John 5:37, 44).

- Fear and judgmental attitudes. When I judge my brother or sister, I no longer see the enormity of my own sin (see Matthew 7:3–5).

- Anger that has gained a foothold. If a prophet has a negative dream about a believer with whom he is angry, he should jettison it along with the other garbage that is polluting his revelatory gift (see James 1:20).

- Paying more attention to the gift than to the Giver, putting more into cultivating His gift to us than into cultivating a close friendship with Him. In the case of the prophet, this also means a loss or contamination of revelation.

- Pressure from people and the temptation to please people, especially when a prophet thinks another person is influential. I have seen even mature prophets rush to the powerful, thinking an invitation from a "powerful one" is as important as an invitation from the all-powerful One. They return disappointed.

The great prophets of the Bible were not impressed by the kings who ruled the earth, but rather by the King who rules heaven and earth. The prophet who was so accurate with me but so wrong with the other pastor had, I believe, fallen into the trap of pleasing the powerful. He thought the pastor was well connected. If he impressed that pastor, maybe the pastor would use his influence to improve the prophet's connections. This is the explanation that makes the most sense to me.

The apostle Paul summed it up this way: "If I were still trying to please people, I would not be a servant of Christ" (Galatians 1:10). Paul knew that one of the quickest ways to fall into deception was to try to please men rather than please God.

How do prophets avoid deception? The same way as all other believers: Pray. Spend time with God. Delight in Him. Obey His voice—no matter who is in the room! Live to please God rather than people. Delight in Him above everything else. Love Him more than all else—especially more than our ministries.

NINE

Growing in Your Prophetic Gift

A denominational church had invited me to speak two nights in a row, the first night on hearing God and the next on healing. This was a little bit of a stretch for this church—I was not a member of their denomination, and hearing God and healing were controversial topics within that denomination.

And now, in front of a thousand people, I was about to be humiliated. I saw a glorious revelation that would set someone free from years of pain. The revelation turned out to be from God, but so did the humiliation!

I took an accomplished prophet with me. The message on hearing God went well. Then we all bowed our heads and waited silently. I received a strong impression, pointed to the back of a full auditorium, and said, "There is someone in the back and on my right who has migraine headaches. You're having one right now. If you'll come down to the front, I think the Lord will heal you."

I was confident, because I was sure this was from the Lord and that He would heal the person. The seconds ticked by. Nobody moved. I repeated the word. Still, nobody moved. People began giving me those pained looks that said, *Oh, he was doing so well until he tried to be a prophet.*

But my prophet friend had mercy on me. He pointed to five men in the second row and said, "Do you know what you five men have in common? You're all pastors. And you're from a denomination that wouldn't approve of your being in a meeting like this."

It was true. My friend went on to deliver a prophetic message to these five men he had never seen before. The audience forgot about my failure as they listened to him tell them the secrets of their hearts.

After the meeting, I was standing down at the front, praying for people. A young man came up to me and said, "That was the most amazing thing I've ever seen!"

"What thing?" I asked.

"You pointed right at me where I was sitting in the back row and said, 'Someone back there has migraines, and you're having one right now.' You were pointing right at me! I've had migraines for several years, and I was having one right then. How could you have known?"

"Wait a minute. You saw me pointing right at you? You didn't come down like I asked? Why not?"

"I don't know. I guess I was just too scared."

"What happened to your migraine?" I asked.

"That's the other amazing thing. As soon as I started walking toward you, it left. They never go away like that. I think I'm healed!"

Accepting the Lord's Discipline

I was right about the migraines, but to all the people, it looked as if I had failed. Since I was coming back the next night, I *could* set the record straight. But what would my motive be in doing that? To bring glory to God or to *me*?

What if it were a test of my heart to reveal my motives for serving God? What if the Lord was disciplining a son He loves (see Hebrews 12:6)? If I refused to accept the discipline, I would just have to take the same test again. A little public humiliation purifies motives for ministry. Paul knew that sometimes God might even let the apostles look as though they had failed the test, when in fact they had passed (see 2 Corinthians 13:7).

Another discipline all prophetic people endure is the "day of small things" (see Zechariah 4:10). Every prophet would like to be able to tell people the most intimate secrets of their hearts, but nobody starts out as a prophet to the nations. This does not mean God never uses a beginner, but it is important to remember that one general word that really is from God, given at the right time, has more power than the most profound human insight. Don't despise humble beginnings. Pursue the Lord more than ministry. You will prosper (see Job 8:5–7).

Praying, Practicing, and Risking

Are you satisfied with the level of gifting in your ministry? If not, remember what James said: "You do not have because you do not ask God" (James 4:2). Pray every day for God to train you in the use of your prophetic gift. Ask Him to increase the accuracy of your gift. Ask Him for specific things regarding your prophetic ministry so that you will have a way of measuring whether you are growing in prophecy. Pray for opportunities to use your gift.

Always pray more for the purifying of your character than for the perfecting of your gift. A great gift alone cannot render great service to God; it takes a great heart! I have seen prophets fall because *they did not have the character to bear their gifts*. God gives us gifts, but He expects us to grow the strength of character to use those gifts to serve Him and not ourselves.

101

Ask the Lord to send you mentors to help you. He has answered this prayer for me by sending me various mentors at different times, and they have played a powerful role in my growth. Ask the Lord to make you a mentor to others as well (see 2 Timothy 2:2), for in teaching and training others, you will grow too.

You can't grow in anything unless you practice. Mature prophets are those "who because of practice have their senses trained to distinguish between good and evil" (Hebrews 5:14 NASB). The only good athlete you will ever see is one who refused to give up. Like that athlete, keep practicing.

One prophetic friend of mine asks the Lord to speak to him about strangers while he's standing in line at the bank or grocery store. If he thinks the Lord has spoken to him about a bank teller, he tests it immediately. He asks a harmless, friendly question: "You don't have a sister named Darla, do you?"

"No, why do you ask?"

"Oh, I must have confused you with someone else."

No problem. He's the only one who knows he missed it.

But with him, it is more likely the bank teller will say, "Yes. How did you know?"

Now he assumes that the Lord really wants to say something to this teller. The risk—and the adventure—begins!

We could just play it safe. But we will never know if we can use the gift when it really counts unless we take the risk. Remember these things:

- No prophetic word can be judged until it is spoken.
- We will never do it perfectly. We will never get it right without first doing it poorly.
- We ask to get the gift. That takes faith.
- We practice to grow in the gift. That takes discipline.
- We risk to bless someone. That takes courage.
- Pray, practice, risk, and find a prophetic community in which you may do all these things.

Prophetic Community

Being around other prophets stimulates us to ask questions, causes us to rethink our own experience, allows us to benefit from the experience of those who are more mature, gives us faith to grow in our gifting, and motivates us to search the Scriptures more diligently.

The best prophetic community was the New Testament church in Antioch, which had both prophets and teachers ministering together (see Acts 13:1–3). Teachers and prophets benefit from each other's strengths.

There are churches like this, and it is worth a diligent search to discover them, for the right prophetic environment helps us keep our focus on Jesus and love one another, and it protects us from deception. The right prophetic community also helps us learn from our inevitable failures.

Learning from Failure

Wise people know that nothing teaches like failure. In every failure, there is a new lesson to be learned. The best way *not* to learn from failure is to blame someone else for it. But I am learning more these days from my own failures and the failures of those close to me than I am from all our successes combined. Let me give you an example.

During my meditation time, I received a new (that is, new to me) insight about why marriages grow cold. I saw clearly the stages of dying love. I also saw a solution for rekindling marital passion. I could not wait to preach on these new insights. I thought the audience would devour these truths with gratitude.

It didn't happen. When the preaching was over, my audience looked depressed. I had wanted to inspire hope and transformation, but I instead had instilled guilt and depression. Why? The easy solution would have been to blame it on the people. I could blame the time of year. It was January. But instead, I simply asked the Lord why the people got depressed after hearing what I thought was a message from Him.

Almost immediately, I got an answer. It went something like this: *You spent all your time describing the death of love. You saved only a few words at the end for its resurrection. If you had reversed this process, the people would have found hope rather than discouragement.*

That made perfect sense. I had spent most of my time on the diagnosis rather than on the cure. This failure taught me to use revelatory insights to their full potential.

Here are some texts that have helped when I have experienced failure. These keep me from blaming others, which in turn keeps me from becoming bitter.

> Search me, O God, and know my heart; test me and know my anxious thoughts. See if there is any offensive way in me, and lead me in the way everlasting (Psalm 139:23–24).

> The wisdom of the prudent is to give thought to their ways (Proverbs 14:8).

> The prudent give thought to their steps (Proverbs 14:15).

> I applied my heart to what I observed and learned a lesson from what I saw (Proverbs 24:32).

I have turned these verses into prayers, and I try to pray them at the beginning of each day. I pray these because the older I get, the more I realize how blind I am to the real causes of my failures. I have found that when I open my heart to the light of the Lord, He grants me merciful revelations that can turn a setback into a step forward.

When you have a revelatory stumble, dust yourself off with the thought that all great spiritual leaders except Jesus have made great mistakes. Each failure helped them grow a little less confident in themselves and more confident in God. Keep a record: What was your latest stumble, and how is it improving you?

Rejoicing in Rejection

Prophets face rejection. And the greater the gifting, the greater the rejection. Rejection starts with the religious leaders. Jesus, the greatest of all the prophets, was "rejected by the elders, chief priests and the teachers of the law" (Mark 8:31). He also warned His followers to expect rejection:

> Blessed are you when people hate you, when they exclude you and insult you and reject your name as evil, because of the Son of Man. Rejoice in that day and leap for joy, because great is your reward in heaven. For that is how their ancestors treated the prophets.
>
> Luke 6:22–23

Why do religious leaders reject a true prophet? Because prophets challenge erroneous traditions and declare new priorities for God's people. Leaders of calcified traditions care more about protecting their position than listening to the voice of God. Of course, they think they are defending orthodoxy, as though God were a member of their denomination and wouldn't dream of violating their "distinctives."

If the Spirit powerfully rests on the prophet, religious leaders will escalate the rejection to persecution. Leaders will accuse him of being unbiblical, divisive, even demonic. No servant of God has carried a great anointing without having to bear these kinds of accusations. Remember that the enemy is the accuser. Don't get mad; pray for and bless these people. Expect God to work in their lives too!

The place of greatest anointing is also the place of greatest controversy. Characteristically in such moves of God, the leaders of the reigning orthodoxy have survived by their political skills for so long that they don't even recognize the prophetic anointing. Jesus told His disciples that enemies would "falsely say all kinds of evil against you because of me" (Matthew 5:11). Sadly, I have seen this prophecy fulfilled too often as Bible-believing leaders have spread gross lies and rumors about prophets whom they feared might take their constituency.

If we get persecuted like this, we're supposed to rejoice. Why? First, it may be a sign of the Spirit resting on us in power (see Matthew 5:11–12).

Second, rejection and persecution can be great teaching tools. They purify our motives in ministry and provide us with opportunities to grow in love (see Matthew 5:43–48). I watched a prophetic friend endure merciless attacks for months. During that time, I did not see any anger eating away at his heart. But the Lord did. He said to my friend, *The measure of your anger toward these men is the measure of your unperceived ambition.* Without that persecution, my friend would never have realized his ambition and how destructive it could be.

Third, persecution can scare away the people pleasers who compromise the authority of divine commandments. People pleasers weaken a ministry by spreading fear and wasting time in unnecessary discussions regarding the ministry's direction. They are usually the first ones to leave when the persecution starts.

Tested by Praise

Praise is a rarer but more difficult test than persecution. Praise frequently seduces. Rejection may cause us to question ourselves, but praise may cause us to feel invulnerable. Listen to what the wisest of men said about praise: "The crucible is for silver and the furnace for gold, and each is tested by the praise accorded him" (Proverbs 27:21 NASB). The greater the prophetic gifting, the greater the testing that comes from praise.

When persecution can't bring us down and praise can't puff us up, we have come a long way down the road toward prophetic maturity. But how does anyone ever get that far?

Prophets have a Counselor to help them keep their focus—the Holy Spirit. Three times, Jesus referred to Him as "the Spirit of truth." The first context in which the Spirit of truth appears, John 14:15–21, concerns loving and obeying Jesus. The second passage is John 15:26–27, which deals with the Spirit's testimony about Jesus. The last context is in John 16:12–16, where the Spirit is said to bring glory to God. The Counselor is called the Spirit of truth because He always points to the Truth, Jesus, and because He reveals the greatest truths to the followers of Jesus. He promotes the love of Jesus, the testimony about Jesus, and the glory of Jesus. Prophetic ministry must always discern what promotes Jesus—first, last, and forever.

This means that the ultimate focus of prophets should never be on their ministries, or even on the needs of the people. If prophets want the guidance of the Holy Spirit, they must focus on Jesus, because that is where the Holy Spirit is focused. By sharing the focus of the Holy Spirit, we get to see the glorious, heart-stopping splendor radiating from Jesus. Persecution, praise, and a thousand other distractions lose their power over us in the presence of His radiant beauty. Everything comes into proper focus when we focus on Jesus.

God sends us His prophets to call us to come closer to that glorious Person who sits at the right hand of the Father, supremely patient as He rules the world by the power of His Word, longing to be closer to you and to me.

POSTSCRIPT

Enjoying the Symphony

Years ago, when I walked into that dingy room with the green carpet and orange plastic chairs, I had no idea the Word of God was waiting for me. I had no idea how much inside me needed to be healed and that only He could heal it. I had no inkling of the journey He had planned for me. I had no idea how much I needed His mercy until I walked into the manger of His mercy.

God's highest purpose for the world was placed in a manger. It has been my experience that His highest purposes for you and for me are still being brought to birth in mangers—places where we least expect to encounter Him. The One who lives in the unapproachable light of glory loves to meet us in the humblest places. Those places reveal His humility and mercy, by which He heals us and to which He calls us.

Until that beautiful fall morning, my knowledge of mangers and humility was mainly limited to what I'd read in theological commentaries. And certainly, that prophetic encounter did not make me a deeply humble person nor give me a profound knowledge of God's present-day mangers. But it did give me a little taste for these things, and it drew me into the prophetic ministry from that day on.

Over the years, I have been greatly rewarded by my pursuit. Prophets have helped me with decisions both in my ministry and in my personal life. But these are not the greatest rewards!

What I've found most wonderful in the prophets is that they are transporters of God's mercy. Their eyes see what ours do not, and His mercy heals what our best efforts cannot. My bitterness is mostly gone now. By the light of prophetic words, I can now understand how events I once viewed as unmitigated disasters fit into the symphony that is my life. Of course, it is an unfinished symphony, but the prophetic trumpets have made it so much richer and more stirring.

I don't know the next movement of my own little symphony, but that is fine with me. I am at peace knowing that His mercy will be directing it. The mystery makes the music even more enjoyable.

I do claim, however, to have a little insight about the direction of the larger symphony of which all believers are a part. The prophetic trumpets are growing stronger, announcing a new movement more powerful than anything you or I have ever heard. The new movement won't be heard until the prophetic trumpets are well integrated with the rest of the instruments. But under God the Conductor's perfect direction, it will come to a marvelous crescendo.

Jack Deere brings practical wisdom to Christians through his teaching ministry, drawing from his experience as a professor at Dallas Theological Seminary, pastor of several churches, and author of bestselling books *Surprised by the Power of the Spirit* and *Surprised by the Voice of God*. He is dean of the extension schools in the Wagner Leadership Institute and executive director of Covenant Ministries International.